Doing What
Scientists Do

P9-BYB-741

Doing What Scientists Do

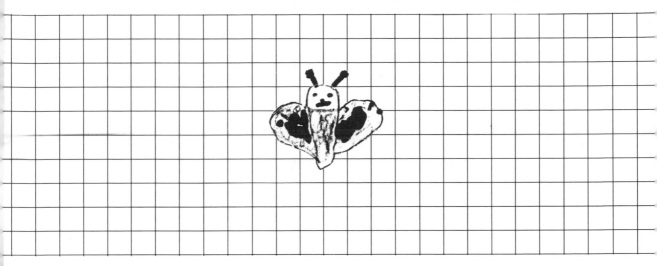

Children Learn to Investigate Their World

Ellen Doris

Heinemann
Portsmouth, New Hampshire

Heinemann
A division of Reed Elsevier Inc.
361 Hanover Street, Portsmouth, NH 03801-3912
Offices and agents throughout the world

© 1991 by The Northeast Foundation for Children.
All rights reserved. No part of this book may be reproduced in any form or by
electronic or mechanical means, including information storage and retrieval
systems, without permission in writing from the publisher, except by a reviewer,
who may quote brief passages in a review.

Every effort has been made to contact the copyright holders and the children and
their parents for permission to reprint borrowed material. We regret any oversights
that may have occurred and would be happy to rectify them in future printings
of this work.
The following have generously given permission to use quotations
from copyrighted works:
Page 19: *Young Geographers* by Lucy Sprague Mitchell. Copyright © 1971 by
Bank Street College of Education. Reprinted by permission.

The three worksheets at the back of this book may be photocopied provided
permission statement is included.

The Northeast Foundation for Children, a private, nonprofit, educational foundation,
works to improve the quality of elementary school teaching through its training
programs, summer workshops, and publications. The Foundation operates a
demonstration school, the Greenfield Center School, which is open to visiting
teachers from October through early April. The Center School provides teachers
the opportunity to see developmentally effective classrooms in action from
kindergarten through eighth grade. A twice yearly publication, *A Newsletter for
Teachers*, is available free of charge. For further information, call or write:
Northeast Foundation for Children, 71 Montague City Road, Greenfield, MA 01301;
(413) 772-2066.

Library of Congress Cataloging-in-Publication Data

Doris, Ellen.
    Doing what scientists do : children learn to investigate their
world / Ellen Doris.
        p.   cm.
    Includes bibliographical references (p.   ).
    ISBN 0-435-08309-0
    1. Science—Study and teaching (Elementary)—United States.
I. Title.
LB1585.3.D67   1991
372.3′5044′0973—dc20   90-48126
                                                                   CIP

Designed by Maria Szmauz.

Printed in the United States of America.

07 06 05 04   EB   12 13 14 15

For Bob

Contents

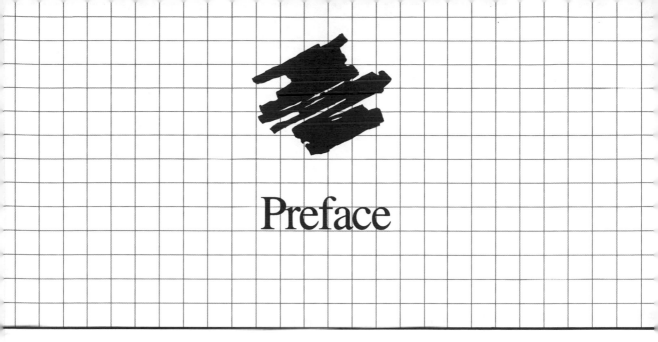

Preface

In most of the classroom examples I have chosen for this book, the children are studying familiar plants and animals. In fact, three chapters focus almost exclusively on the study of a pet guinea pig. This heavy emphasis on the biological sciences is not meant to suggest, however, that work in other areas is unsuitable for elementary school children. I have found topics in chemistry, physics, and the earth sciences to be of great interest to children, and I have enjoyed watching as they discover what sinks and what floats, what strange properties are exhibited by a simple mixture of cornstarch and water, and what rocks look like on the inside. Although, for many teachers, biology offers a familiar place to begin, the approach to science illustrated here can help teachers work successfully with children in any branch of science.

Acknowledgments

My ideas about teaching science have been evolving for longer than I can say. I am grateful to the many people who, knowingly or not, have influenced my thinking, teaching, and finally, my writing. In particular, I thank:

Sharon Dunn, who served as project coordinator for this book;

Chip Wood, who oversaw this project in its early phases and also served as a reader; as well as contributed photographs;

Ruth Charney and Bob Strachota, whose ongoing work with me has helped me to understand and to write;

Merle Bruno, for her input as a reader;

John Doris and Susan Mitchell for suggesting references and additions to the bibliography;

Nancy Ratner for her skillful and sensitive editing;

Lucy Matteau who carefully typed my endless drafts and final manuscript;

Marlyn Clayton, Bill Forbes, Bob Strachota, Chip Wood, and Ken Williams who contributed photographs;

Timmy Sheyda for his documentation of classroom work;

Barney Balch for the dinoflagellate story;

Chuck Meyers and Jed Proujansky for obtaining permission to use the quotations and children's work that illustrate this book;

Toby Gordon and Cheryl Kimball, editors at Heinemann, and designer Maria Szmauz for their many contributions;

and the members of the Editorial Review Board, Northeast Foundation for Children.

I also thank my colleagues at the Greenfield Center School, from whom I have learned a great deal, and the teachers I've met through workshops who have shared both their insights and struggles with me. And, of course, fond thanks to the children who have explored science with me, and contributed their experiences and products to this book.

Finally, I am deeply grateful to family and friends for their support and encouragement.

Introduction

One snowy Saturday morning, I sat with a group of elementary school teachers in a science workshop. We reflected on the question I had posed: "If, through teaching science, you could give the children in your classroom just one or two important things, what would you give them?" The responses were clear, thoughtful, and sure:

"I'd give children the freedom to question!"

"I want them to be more aware of the natural world . . . and for that awareness to enhance, not diminish, their sense of wonder."

"I'd like them to develop a healthy respect and responsibility for nature."

"I'd give them the eagerness to investigate! And patience—to be able to wait and look."

"When they come upon something new, I want them to have lots of different avenues open for learning about it."

"Curiosity!"

"I want them to know that their teacher does not have all the answers!"

"Good communication is important to me. I want them to be able to summarize what they've seen and to share it."

"I want them to feel that there's an interesting world out there, and that they have access to that world."

Each of us was identifying something deeply important. We valued the children we taught and the world around us. We wanted the connection between these children and that world to be marked by curiosity, awareness, respect, eagerness, patience, responsibility, interest, and wonder. We wanted these children to be able to investigate, learn, and communicate. We spoke with conviction about the value of science study at the elementary school level.

I thought back to the previous evening when we had collected for the first time and introduced ourselves. Our reasons for participating in this workshop varied:

"Frankly, I don't teach science. When I was in school, I always thought science was boring. And I still think it's boring! But I'm ready for someone to convince me it's not."

"I do lots of science projects with my second graders. They love science. But I feel I could do more. I'm ready for something new."

"I have no science background at all. I really don't feel prepared to work with the fifth and sixth graders that I teach."

"I feel that kids come to school with so much interest. They're always bringing in their rocks and caterpillars and seashells. I want to know how to help them develop that interest."

We were all struggling, at one level or another, to bring our ideals and the realities of our classrooms closer together. We didn't lack purpose; that was clear. We believed that science could be an exciting and meaningful part of classroom work for children and for us. But what, and how, to change? Some of us felt the need for drastic overhaul. One teacher exclaimed, "I've been given a science textbook to teach from. *Twenty* chapters! The expectation is that we'll cover all twenty in the third grade this year! Why, we won't even have time to stop for questions!"

Others felt their lessons were on the right track but that they could be doing more. "What is it that causes some kids to be so interested in science?" a fifth-grade teacher wondered. "Is it age, or culture, or adult response, or personality? I see some kids who just can't seem to get enough—and others who just can't seem to get going! I'd like to see all of them engaged and involved."

This gap between teacher's convictions and classroom reality parallels the gap between what theoreticians, researchers, and program developers recommend and what is actually practiced in elementary schools across the nation.

Although the National Science Resources Center's 1986 National Conference on the Teaching of Science in Elementary Schools recommended placing participatory activities at the center of the elementary science curriculum, it was found that even in 1989, "less than two percent of the children in our elementary schools have an opportunity to participate in an inquiry-oriented elementary science program" (NSRC 1988, 1989).

The National Association for the Education of Young Children has defined appropriate teaching practice in science as follows:

> Discovery science is a major part of the curriculum, building on children's natural interest in the world. Science projects are experimental and exploratory and encourage active involvement of every

child. The science program takes advantage of natural phenomena such as the outdoors, and the classroom includes many plants and pets for which children provide care daily. Through science projects and field trips, children learn to plan; to dictate and/or write their plans; to apply thinking skills such as hypothesizing, observing, experimenting, and verifying; and many science facts related to their own experience. (1988, 74)

This description is consistent with many teachers' opinions about the value of "hands-on" instruction. A recent national survey reported that "approximately two-thirds of elementary science teachers and more than three-fourths of secondary science teachers indicated that laboratory-based science classes are more effective than non-laboratory classes" (*Report of the 1985–86 National Survey of Science and Mathematics Education* 1987, 52). Yet, in actual classroom practice, teachers have moved away from laboratory classes. Only 57 percent of kindergarten through third-grade and 45 percent of fourth- through sixth-grade teachers surveyed had used hands-on activities in their most recent science lesson—a drop from 67 percent and 54 percent respectively, as reported in a 1977 survey (*Report of the 1985–86 National Survey of Science and Mathematics Education* 1987, 49).

Support for "hands-on" instruction is not new. In the seventies, Piaget recommended "the use of active methods which give broad scope to the spontaneous research of the child or adolescent and require that every new truth to be learned be rediscovered or at least reconstructed by the student, and not simply imparted to him" (1976, 15–16). In the years that have passed, how many children have spent a significant part of each school day involved in "spontaneous research," able to "discover or reconstruct by rediscovery" (Piaget 1976, 20) the nature of the world around them?

There are several reasons for the continued distance between educational theory and actual practice, between teacher visions and classroom reality. Some have roots in teachers' own experiences as science students. Their memories of elementary and high school science experiences are revealing:

"Science? In elementary school? I don't remember anything. I guess there wasn't any."

"I remember in the fifth grade, our teacher borrowed a huge telescope from the local university, and invited everyone to a 'star party.' I remember standing with my father on the dark playing fields behind the school, and looking up just in time to see a flock of geese cross the sky, silent and silver with reflected moonlight."

"I just remember that you had to hurry. You had to finish your experiment in forty minutes. You had to read the procedure carefully. If you didn't, the experiment went wrong. If anything went wrong, then you'd be out of time."

"I could never understand physics! The teacher would try to explain, but still I didn't get it. Then he'd be angry. I felt it was my fault that I didn't get it.''

"My teacher took us to a nature camp for a week. There was a marsh there, and we compared core samples from different parts of the marsh. I thought the variegated layers of earth were beautiful. It was exciting being an investigator! Back at school, though, the samples went on the science table. I remember the rule was 'No touching.' And then I don't remember any more science that year.''

"The thing I remember is dissecting a frog. The class was really hyped. The funny thing is that I don't remember anything I learned. Just that we did it.''

For many teachers the relationship between these early experiences and present classroom situations is obvious. Those who remember choosing their own projects, building, experimenting, and going on field trips with an enthusiastic teacher are often anxious to provide similar experiences for their students. Those who remember confusing procedures, boring textbooks, or pressure to come up with the right answer are often anxious about their capacity to understand and teach science. This anxiety has led some teachers to rely heavily on textbooks or "ready-made" science curricula. Although they did not benefit from this approach as students, they lack the confidence needed to implement something different. Others avoid teaching science altogether in an effort to avoid repeating poor instruction. Lack of appropriate models and feelings of incompetence can keep teachers from realizing the goals they establish.

Even if teachers have a sense of comfort and ability in science, access to appropriate materials and resources, and a willingness to try something new, there may still be difficulties. A teacher describing the status of science education in her district confided:

> Our school district spent hundreds of dollars on science materials for the primary grades. We tried a unit on balancing for a few years. Then we hid the kit in the back of a storage closet and we're hoping our principal will just forget all about it! I'm the only one out of six teachers who'd even consider using it again! The kids started off okay—they really liked using the balances. But by the end of the first week all the nuts and bolts and macaroni were mixed up together, and lots of it had been lost. Balances were breaking. Some kids were really interested, but some were bored or fooling around.

Teaching science in a classroom of twenty or thirty children requires careful attention to many things. In addition to acquiring a basic understanding of science, teachers must think about specific content and consider the special needs and interests of many children as they plan their curriculum. They must develop techniques that will foster inquiry, plan and maintain an effective physical environment, and deal with issues of management and discipline. Having appropriate materials is not enough to make a science program work, for the way we introduce materials will determine where the nuts and bolts and macaroni will be at the end of the week, and the way that we ask questions and comment on children's work will affect their interest and focus.

In this book I present an approach to teaching science at the elementary school level that will help children feel interested in the world around them and able to find out about that world. Here are the beliefs that guide my approach:

Science is a process of inquiry and investigation. It is a way of thinking and acting, not just a body of knowledge to be acquired by memorizing facts and principles.

Applying what we know about child development contributes to science teaching. Understanding how children at different ages think and work is important in planning, interpreting, and responding to children's science work.

Children learn through their own activity. As apprenticing scientists, they learn about their world by observing, describing, questioning, and searching for answers.

Teachers can also be active investigators. Teachers can share their own curiosity and interest in the world around them, puzzling about phenomena and exploring along with the children.

A balance between structure and freedom in the classroom is important. By balancing open-ended exploration and focused investigation, teachers create a stable classroom environment, which can incorporate activities initiated by the children as well as those teachers have designed or directed themselves.

Familiar, everyday phenomena provide a rich focus for science study. Through direct experience with the plants, animals, and objects that surround them, children can begin thinking scientifically and drawing conclusions from firsthand observations, rather than relying primarily on books, lectures, or films for information.

Each class member has an important contribution to make. Science should not be restricted to students in "gifted and talented" programs, or reserved as a reward for children who can finish their assigned work quickly. Science is a valuable part of the curriculum for everyone.

Collaboration is important—between teacher and students, between students, between members of the class and people outside it. Just as scientists thrive on the exchange of ideas, children also benefit from working cooperatively.

All too often, when teachers put away the textbooks and try to implement a "laboratory" or "hands-on" approach to teaching science, the classroom management problems that arise cause them to give up in frustration. Some may continue with their efforts, but feel uncertain about what it is that children are learning. The open-ended questions and opportunities for independent experimentation a teacher provides may prove to be exciting challenges for some children, while others flounder, or wander, or can't quite make sense of things. Some teachers working to improve the quality of their science programs may feel stymied by their own negative feelings about science or by a limited background in science. Others may struggle to find teaching strategies that will allow them to implement their ideas. I hope to address these problems here and help teachers bring classroom reality closer to their visions of what elementary science can be.

Beginning

Teaching science begins with planning.

For me, the first stage of planning is a time for questioning, considering, remembering, daydreaming, and talking with other teachers. Before tackling the details of scheduling, preparing worksheets, grouping children, and sequencing lessons, I try to answer some fundamental questions. What is science? How do children learn? What do I hope children will gain through their work in science? My answers to these questions affect the way I need to work with children in the classroom.

This may seem a rather philosophical place to begin, given certain realities of teaching. September will bring a classroom full of children. A thousand things must be considered in preparation for that first day: the room needs to be set up; materials and supplies located, ordered, or organized; programs scheduled; and meetings attended. But first, I need to establish my sense of purpose and direction. Specific decisions about what, how, and where to study will follow from my convictions about science and teaching.

My answers to the questions posed above are offered here as one perspective on teaching elementary school science. They provide the framework that underlies the specific approach described in this book. Each teacher will develop an individual perspective based on experience, priorities, attitudes about science, and goals for children.

What Is Science?

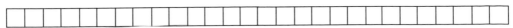

Science is a way of thinking and acting (Figure 1–1). It is a "process of inquiry, resulting in a body of systematized knowledge" (Victor and

Lerner 1971, 77). In the words of Eleanor Duckworth, "the essence of science is not the simple statement of principles, but rather the struggle to find out about the material world" (1978, 1) (Figure 1–2).

My interest is in bringing science, in all its complexity, into the classroom. I want to see children actively engaged, doing the work that scientists do. I want them to see that the body of knowledge that results from scientific investigation is continually evolving and expanding as new technologies, insights, and connections cause us to revise and refine our ideas. Unfortunately, in many elementary schools, the image persists of scientific knowledge as a static collection of truths. A first-grade teacher, reflecting on her own early education, said, "I thought learning science just meant memorizing all these facts! Scientists were the people who had all the answers."

From a scientist's point of view, however, answers are often elusive. A scientist once told me a story that began with early twentieth-century paleobotanists, whose work was taxonomic: describing, naming, and classifying the many species of fossil dinoflagellates. Dinoflagellates are microscopic, one-celled organisms, often grouped with the algae and considered plants, although, prior to 1900, they were assigned to the animal kingdom.[1] Today most dinoflagellates live in the ocean, where they swim propelled by their two little whiplike flagella. Some are luminescent, and when the water surrounding them is disturbed (by the action of waves or by splashing feet), the light they produce causes the water to sparkle and glow. Others, when present in great numbers, form the "red tide" responsible for fish kills and the closing of shellfish beds.

In the early 1900s many fossil dinoflagellate species were described, classified, and assigned Latin names, which enabled scientists worldwide to communicate without confusion. Decades later, geologists studying sediment cores from the ocean bottom found what appeared to be dinoflagellates in their samples. They studied these new additions to the fossil record and worked out a complete taxonomy for them. As before, this taxonomy was based on the geological nomenclature, which referred to fossilized remains of organisms, most of them extinct.

Meanwhile, biologists, culturing "red-tide" dinoflagellates in the laboratory, noticed that they had a life cycle involving several stages. At times they swam in water as motile, flagellated organisms, and at other times they lost the ability to move, "encysted," and settled into the bottom sediments. Later, they would "excyst" and swim around again. Of course, biologists gave these "red-tide" species labels within biological nomenclature.

Geologists continued to study fossil dinoflagellates and found that

---

[1]Some scientists today continue to consider dinoflagellates plants, while others place them in neither plant nor animal kingdom, preferring another kingdom altogether.

Figure 1–1	**Scientists in the classroom**

Figure 1–2	**"The essence of science . . . is the struggle to find out about the material world."**

they occurred in surface sediments as well as deeper, older layers. This prompted one geologist to bring some into the laboratory. Amazingly, these "fossils" excysted, developed flagella, and began to swim around!

This discovery must have been, at the very least, unnerving. And it created certain problems. Geologists now understood that the dinoflagellates in marine sediments were encysted forms and not fossils. But of course, geologists still used the species names in the geological nomenclature. Meanwhile, biologists referred to the "red-tide" dinoflagellates by their biological species names. Eventually geologists and biologists comparing notes determined that the dinoflagellates they were studying were, in fact, the same species, known by different names. Important connections could now be made, but formidable technical problems arose as well. Years of research had been conducted and papers published, some referring to a particular dinoflagellate by one name, some by another. How could all this research be interpreted without confusion? How should new work be described?

This story, like most stories of scientific discovery, has no real end. It is the story of scientific research evolving and changing over nearly a century. But this research revolved around "facts" that were not as firm as the "facts" that many of us were schooled to think made up the fabric of science. Creatures thought to be animals were determined to be plants by some, animals by others, while still others maintained that they were neither. Organisms that were understood to be fossils turned out to be very much alive and capable of swimming around in the laboratory. A fossil dinoflagellate known as species "A" to a geologist turned out to be none other than the living species "23" familiar to a biologist. Just where is the truth? It all seems to depend upon whom you consult and which question you ask.

When we do science we search for answers, but we seldom stop in any particular place for long. Ideas are formed, reviewed, and revised. Interpretations vary. Questions sometimes lead to answers, and invariably lead to other questions.

How Do Children Learn?

Many different theories describe aspects of children's growth and development, including how children learn. This mass of theory and research can provide valuable insight into the needs and abilities of children at different ages, helping us plan and reflect upon classroom work. My own work has been strongly influenced by several theories of child development, as well as research on teaching and learning.[2]

Exploring new ideas about education, testing them against our experience, deciding which ideas to discard and which to try to put to use can be an invigorating and exciting part of teaching. It can also seem overwhelming: developing a thorough familiarity with varied and complicated theories of learning and development and "keeping up" with current research while continuing to meet the demands of a full-time teaching job is a practical impossibility.

Fortunately, we can proceed with science instruction anyway, since children have a way of letting us know what it is they understand and what they need. Blank looks, laughter, frustration, and excitement instruct us as well as theories of development and models of learning. Theory is based on research. We can, in effect, work as researchers in the classroom, observing children carefully, listening to what they say, noting when our responses seem to baffle them and when we help them take a step forward. Science textbooks may offer us information to present or questions to raise, but only our careful attention to children will enable us to gather information about what they find interesting or puzzling, which ideas they understand and which ones confuse them.

Many opportunities to apply our understanding arise in a day. For example, five- and six-year-olds are quick to raise questions:

"Can I mix these paints together?"

"Can we put these beads in the water table?"

"My flower needs more water. Can I fill the jar all the way to the top?"

"Can we get the guinea pig out and read him a story?"

For the most part, my answers to such questions are simple:

"You want to see what happens? Sure, go ahead."

"Your flower needs water? You can take care of that."

There are, of course, other possible responses:

"If you mix the paints, then you'll be all out of blue when you need it."

"These beads are made of wood. So you can imagine what's going to happen to them in the water table."

"Your flower can get plenty of water already. See, the stem reaches down to the bottom where the water is."

"Do you really think our guinea pig can understand stories?" But I bite my tongue when I think of these (Figures 1–3).

With this age group, it is important to reward children's initiative. The projects they initiate may not make much sense to me. I don't see why a flower needs water "right up to the top," and I miss the colorful

---

[2]My work as a teacher has been influenced by a slow and continual influx of ideas from theoretical works, research findings, ideas and insights shared by colleagues. Often these glimpses into developmental and educational theories have nourished my interest in my work. Other times they have helped me to understand a classroom failure and to plan more successfully.

| Figure 1–3 | Talking to the guinea pig |

tempera paintings that give way to those brownish-gray, grayish-brown, brownish-brown, and mauve creations that are the end result of some paint-mixing experiments (Figure 1–4). But if I want children to feel able to try out their own ideas and develop a sense of purpose, I need to support them with a "yes" when it is safe and reasonably practical to do so. I work to help children think and act scientifically, but try to remember the limits that young children's thinking imposes. Sometimes, children can carefully report actual observations of the guinea pig: he drinks water, he eats, he has no tail. But other times they may report that he wants to hear a story. The paints can be mixed, and the beads dropped in the water table, and children will be quick to note what happens. However, expecting children's predictions to match the actual results of these experiments is unrealistic, as is expecting that imagining the outcome (these beads are made of wood, so they'll probably float) is a substitute for actually carrying out the proposed action.

Although older children also initiate projects, their thinking is more sophisticated. They are able to plan and reason in new ways, make comparisons, devise simple investigations, and draw conclusions about their observations. One day during cleanup time eight-year-old Carrie was sweeping the floor and bumped into the art table, knocking a soda bottle full of wildflowers onto the floor. It broke. I went to clean it up and Carrie moved closer to watch. I gingerly picked up a large piece of glass with "deposit" still visible in raised letters. Before I could

| Figure 1–4 | **Young children experiment with paint at the easel** |

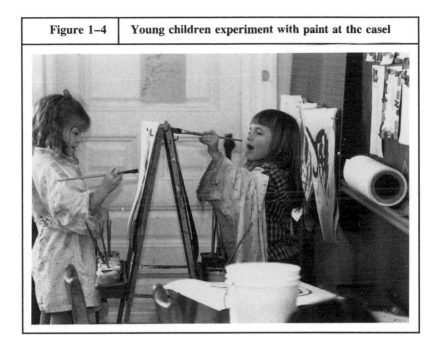

place it in the paper bag with the other fragments, Carrie interrupted, "Can I have that?"

"This broken glass? What do you want it for?"

"Well, you know sea glass? Sometimes it has writing like that. I was wondering, maybe we could make sea glass."

I was intrigued by her idea, but concerned about the mess. "Let me finish cleaning this up. I don't want anyone to get hurt! If you go get me a box, I'll wrap this piece up so we can store it safely. Then after cleanup time we can talk more about your idea."

Later on, I inquired, "How do you think sea glass is made?"

"Well," Carrie began, "in the ocean, there's water, and salt, and the glass gets worn smooth."

"So the water and salt get to work on the glass?"

"I think so," Carrie nodded tentatively.

"And what is it you'd like to try with this glass?" I asked.

"Well, we could put it, no, a little piece of it, with some water. Maybe it would change."

"Do you need any special kind of water?" I questioned.

"Well, we can't get ocean water!" Carrie laughed. "We could put regular water in, and some salt."

"Those are both things we have at school," I offered. "Then what would you do?"

"Look at it every day. I could see if anything's happened."

I went over her steps. "So you'll put a small piece of this bottle in a container with water and salt and watch to see if it changes to sea glass?''

Carrie nodded. We figured out a safe way to break off a small piece of the glass for her experiment, and she got to work setting it up.

Again, things could have proceeded differently. When the bottle broke, all I saw was a dangerous mess. I wanted it cleaned up and safe. When Carrie said, ''Can I have that?'' my first thought was, ''Of course not! You could get hurt!'' But I felt I should at least find out what was on her mind. When she proposed making sea glass, I was intrigued, but did not simply respond: ''You want to make sea glass? Sure, give it a try!''

Eight-year-olds are full of ideas and quick to suggest projects.

''We want to write a book. It's going to be about all of the different birds of prey in the world.''

''I think our class should build a model of the pond we've been visiting. A scale model! We'll make it just like the real one, with all the ducks and geese, and the windmill and trees and . . .''

''Our group is writing a play.''

''I want to figure out how things fly.''

It is important for them, as well as younger children, to pursue projects they initiate. Experimenting, collecting, constructing, and reading all hold rewards. However, if I simply encourage every big idea that is proposed, some children may be unable to follow through with their ideas; they may fail to anticipate all the steps necessary to achieve satisfactory results. Feelings of failure or frustration may result, rather than a sense of competence. With help, children can draw on their ability to think about real situations, clarifying questions, anticipating some problems, formulating plans. A helpful response to an eight-year-old's proposal is often: ''Tell me more about your idea. How do you think you could get to work on that? What will you need? Who can help?''

I have found that in my science work with children, it helps to keep in mind a few basic ideas about how children learn. These ideas help me formulate and carry out my plans in the classroom. And they are ideas that, should I forget, a child will surely help me remember.

Children learn by doing. Children gain knowledge as they act upon objects, interact with other people, and try to make sense of their experience (Piaget in Wadsworth 1979). As a science teacher, I need to keep in mind that children learn most effectively as a result of their own efforts, acting, experimenting, and struggling to make sense of their experiences. Few children can truly understand a lecture or come to ''know'' the natural world by reading about it in a textbook. They need real opportunities for direct investigation.

Constructing knowledge requires collaboration. (Piaget 1976, 95, 107–8) Again and again, I have watched children build ideas as they work together on a project, as in the following example, when Bobby, age seven, was explaining some recent developments in his class's investigation of pond animals.

"Come look at our caddisflies," he urged.

I peered into a glass dish housing a number of these insect larvae, each inhabiting a case it had constructed of tiny bits of leaves, reeds, and other aquatic vegetation (see Figure 1–5).

"See what they're doing?" Bobby pointed. "Ricky was the first one that noticed that. Now we've all been seeing it."

Several of the caddisflies seemed to be bumping into one another, sometimes even climbing atop one another's cases. This was accompanied by lots of up and down movements of their tiny heads.

"That is interesting behavior!" I agreed.

"At first we thought they were fighting. That was Kevin's idea, I think. Because it looks like they might be fighting. Then Heather had a different idea. She thought maybe when they climb on top of each other like that, they're mating. But then Terry said no, these caddisflies are just babies really; the grownups look like moths or something. So we decided they probably weren't mating.

Figure 1–5	Caddisfly drawn by eight-year-old boy	Figure 1–6	Children observe caddisfly behavior

"Then I had the theory that one of them is eating the other. Not really eating it, but you know, eating its shell. They move their heads up and down and eat. But now Jenny has a new theory. She thinks they get things from other caddisflies' shells, and they put them on their own shell. We're trying to find out which theory is right" (see Figure 1–6, preceding page).

Collaboration also benefits adult learners. Teachers at workshops are often surprised and delighted at the change that occurs when they "partner up" to do an observation (Figure 1–7), or when one working group becomes aware of what another one is doing: "I got really interested in the inside of the turtle shell, but before I saw Patricia turn it over, I was just looking at the top—the way it had been set out on the table. And inside I discovered what I think is the backbone! I never thought turtles had backbones!" "When Pam and I joined up with the other group, our work was much more fun! And I learned more about these liquids we're experimenting with, because other people kept giving me ideas for new things to try!"

In teaching science, I try to create opportunities for collaboration. Scientists may spend long hours working alone, but they also rely on others. They read each other's publications, duplicate each other's experiments, team up to do research, solve problems, and discuss ideas. This balance of independent and team work can be a model for the classroom.

Figure 1–7	Teachers experiment with liquids at workshop

Children's behavior and thinking develop over time. Children at different ages (or at different stages of development) have characteristic ways of thinking and behaving. Particular issues may be important at one age and not at another. Children learn best when teachers take into account the particular characteristics of their age group.

Children are individuals. Individual children have different strengths, interests, needs, and learning styles. Some children benefit especially from structured situations with clear guidelines, while others thrive in more open-ended learning environments. Even on a task as seemingly well defined as drawing or writing about an object on a science worksheet, individual approaches emerge. Children learn best when teachers appreciate the individuality of each student and teach accordingly.

Children are continually revising their understanding of the world. Knowledge builds on other knowledge. As we learn about the world, we experience new things, test out ideas, make new connections, and alter our picture of "the way things work." In the classroom, different children will often be at different levels of understanding a particular situation or phenomenon. We must proceed from each child's own level. This, I believe, is part of what educators mean when they say we must "start where children are." As we proceed, we must keep in mind that mistakes are part of learning and that learning is an ongoing process. Children may discard one misconception for another more refined, but still false, idea (Piaget 1976, 21). As teachers we may panic as we observe this process in our classrooms; if the children, at the end of a unit of study, report misunderstandings, we may fear we haven't taught them well enough. In fact, they will leave each year (as will we) with certain things well understood, and other things only partially understood. We must provide children with the time, materials, and other resources that will allow them to build up a network of ideas about the world, trusting that they will add to that network throughout their lives.

Feelings are part of learning. There are emotional, attitudinal, and aesthetic aspects of learning, as well as intellectual ones. Rachel Carson, writer and naturalist, suggested that emotions "pave the way for the child to want to know":

> Once the emotions have been aroused—a sense of the beautiful, the excitement of the new and the unknown, a feeling of sympathy, pity, admiration or love—then we wish for knowledge about the object of our emotional response. Once found it has lasting meaning. (1956, 45)

Taking feelings into account is an important part of "starting where children are."

What Do I Hope Children Will Gain Through Their Work in Science?

My most basic goal is to help children feel interested in the world around them and able to find out about that world. The task of helping children develop interest, curiosity, or wonder (Figure 1–8) is especially important to me. It is also especially complicated. Often children become immediately engaged—focused, lively, questioning, thoughtful —when presented with materials for building, or animals or objects for studying, but not always. Many teachers have had the experience of providing materials to children and hearing responses such as ''I'm bored!'' ''Oh, this again,'' ''So what's the big deal about looking for birds?'' or ''I'm done.'' Other children may explore materials briefly then move on, or may appear aimless in their work, rather than engaged.

Many factors may be responsible. Children live in a fast-paced, sometimes dazzling, world. For example, television programs entertain, but demand little of the viewer. Episodes are designed for short attention spans or rely on sirens, explosions, car chases, or other extraordinary drama to keep children involved. Compared with this glittering world,

Figure 1–8	**''he chased after my hand when I pet it!''**

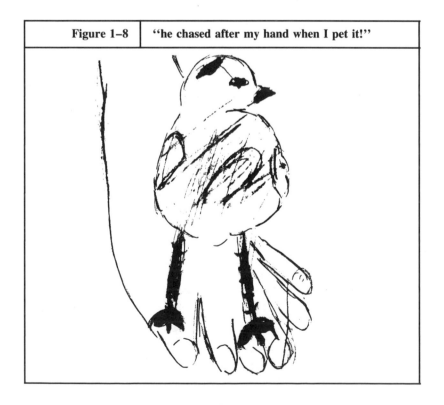

a cricket can appear, on first glance, rather dull. Some children may simply lack the active strategies required to investigate a problem. Other children may have learned a passive approach to school work; if questions have always been framed by the teacher, students may not know how, or trust that they are free, to come up with their own questions. Interest requires, I believe, a confidence that you can have an idea and figure something out for yourself. If questions rarely lead to understanding, then some children may conclude that it is better not to be curious.

In 1934, educator Lucy Sprague Mitchell described the situation of the children she taught:

> Modern children are born into an appallingly complicated world. A three-year-old in a city environment may be whisked to his steam-heated nursery in an electric elevator, fed from supplies which are ordered by telephone, sent up in a dumb-waiter and stored in an electric refrigerator; he may be taken to a hole in the sidewalk and borne rapidly on an underground train to a distant place. The forces which move his elevator, warm his nursery, extend his mother's voice to a grocery store, cool his milk, propel the subway train, are complicated and difficult to understand not only at three, at six, at nine, but even at forty. Most of them are hidden from him: indeed, they may be hidden from his parents. He lives in a world of end-products with the functioning causes largely concealed. He is likely to grow up so used to unexplained end-products that he does not form the habit of seeking for causes, for underlying relationships. Which is a round-about way of saying, that so far as this functioning aspect of his environment is concerned, he is likely to grow up without thinking, without opportunity for experimentation. . . . Nowadays a country child as well as his city and suburban brothers is likely to grow up without understanding or even questioning many familiar things—without thinking so far as the functioning aspect of his world is concerned. And be it said once more, the grown-ups closely associated with these modern children may accept their environment with an attitude almost equally unchallenging. (1971, 12–13)

Through science work, we can help children develop an interest in the ordinary, yet extraordinary, world around them and reward themselves with understanding.

I urge teachers to read about and discuss child development, psychology, and research that relates to science education (see the Bibliography, particularly section 16). I also urge teachers to be open-minded, critically reflective, and flexible in their efforts to understand and apply research and theory. In child study, just as in scientific observation, ideas and theories form a framework that can often help us to interpret what we see. The danger, of course, is that our preconceptions will so influence our observations that we will not truly see what is before us. Theories are imperfect attempts to describe patterns and relationships. We must use them only selectively and in concert with the knowledge we develop about each individual child we teach.

2

Creating an Environment for Science in the Classroom

In trying to create a successful environment for science, I keep the following ideas in mind:

Excitement, wonder, questions, and surprises are a part of science. I need to be attentive to what sparks interest, what is frustrating, and what is rewarding.

Children can become scientists in the classroom. They will learn best if they can observe and study natural phenomena directly (rather than just memorize facts or hear about work others have done). This does not mean that children need a laboratory filled with expensive equipment in order to work, or that eight-year-olds will be able to reason about hypothetical situations that have no connection to their concrete experiences. It does mean that children need to be involved in direct exploration of the world around them.

Children need plenty of time to work! Observing, investigating and developing and testing ideas all take time. It is better to pursue one question or topic in depth than to try to cover lots and lots of material. One year, I spent from September through December studying crickets with a class of seven- and eight-year-olds. Another year, we studied birds from September through June! Five- and six-year-olds began with their guinea pig one fall. He remained the center of science work for almost two months.

Children need to be able to work together. Partnerships, small-group, and whole-class activities contribute both to the pleasure and productivity of the class.

Children will draw from a given experience in ways different from adults and from each other. This happens because of developmental differences, individual experiences, and unique personalities. I try to create science experiences that offer a range of possible directions and outcomes, and to accept various ways of working and thinking.

Particular experiences should be geared to a child's age and experience. I choose activities that reflect both my own interests and the children's interests and abilities.

The Importance of the Room and Its Contents in Creating a Place for Science

Where will science happen? Of course, science can happen anywhere—outside, at the window, at the rabbit cage, or at a child's desk—but, even so, I believe we need a special area of the room for science, and this is important for a number of reasons.

First, making space for science is a visible statement of our priorities. Anyone who enters the room and looks around can see that science is an important part of our work in this class.

Second, if a space is always available for science work, children can choose to work on science whenever they have time. If a space is available and the children are taught how to work in that space with purpose and independence, they will initiate science study in ways that are meaningful for them—ways I may or may not have considered. Many children have taught me this. One year it was a pair of seven-year-old boys. That fall our class studied crickets. We kept them in glass aquariums on the science table, fed them dry dog food, and watered them with tiny sponge-plugged bottles. Miles and Cory came to school each morning, stored their coats and lunches, and headed for the science table. They had a regular morning vigil and would again take time for a quick look on the way to their reading group or just before cleaning up. During our quiet work period in the afternoon, they often chose to go to the science table and look some more.

During that fall there were many teacher-structured science times, with everyone in the class involved in observing, talking, drawing, and writing about our crickets (Figure 2–1). The self-chosen, independent work of these two seven-year-olds differed from teacher-structured work. No records were kept; no particular questions were articulated; there were no schedules, no deadlines, no book research. It was their time to watch and listen and to pursue their own interest in their own way. They approached this work with affection and dedication.

Figure 2–1	A "krikit"

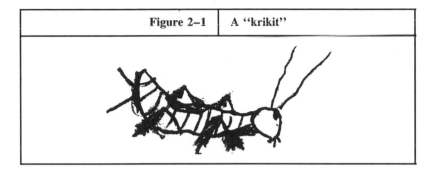

Were they learning anything? I am convinced that they were. At times I'd be working nearby, watching a group paint with watercolors or helping someone with a reading assignment. Miles would motion for me to come and take a look: "See how this one is moving her head? We think that's how she eats."

During whole-class discussions, questions were often raised about the behavior we observed.

"I saw one cricket put its antenna in its mouth!" an amazed eight-year-old reported.

"Lots of them do that," corroborated Cory.

"Maybe they're eating their antennae!" suggested another classmate.

"I don't think so," Cory replied thoughtfully, "because later, it seems like they still have their whole antennae. The antennae don't keep getting shorter."

I was struck by how often these two boys made similar contributions to our discussions, remembering an observation or providing useful data as we considered a hypothesis. Equally important to me was that they were learning to work with independence and purpose, making choices about the direction their learning would take.

A permanent place for science means it is easier for children to be involved in long-term projects. If children have to put objects or experiments away and out of sight at the end of a work period, ongoing involvement requires anticipation, scheduling, unpacking. Young children are not usually able to anticipate and organize to the degree that would enable them to follow through on ideas, so many questions remain unanswered or forgotten.

Another reason I like permanent work and display space for science is that it helps children be aware of and learn from one another's work. Alex, age five, taught me this when he proudly brought me his second drawing of the guinea pig. The previous week he had not been too pleased with his work (Figure 2–2A). He had explained with a shrug, "I don't know how to draw guinea pigs yet."

Figure 2–2A	Alex's guinea pig: First attempt

Name of Scientist ___Alex_____

I looked at _____

——— A picture of what I saw ——————————

I noticed _____

_____

_____

_____

Figure 2–2B	Alex's guinea pig: Second attempt

Name of Scientist **Alex** _____

I looked at _____

—— A picture of what I saw ——

I noticed _____

_____

_____

_____

Looking at his second attempt (Figure 2–2B) I commented, "Alex! You really show the shape of his body in this drawing."

"I used to make them look like people," he explained, "'cause I didn't know how to draw the bodies of animals yet."

"I notice how much your work has changed," I said. "How did you learn?"

He pointed to another child's work on the science bulletin board. "I looked at Joel's. He didn't say about how to do it but when I looked, I could tell."

In planning a space, I need to keep in mind the kind of work I want children to be doing and the characteristics and needs of my class. I also have to factor in the space available in the room, the location of other work areas, the furniture and supplies available to me.

Supplies

The essential materials and equipment you will need are easy to come by:

table or desks

chairs

a few containers for housing visiting animals

crayons, pencils, and colored pencils

blank paper or worksheets

Helpful, but certainly not necessary, are

hand lenses

clipboards

a microscope (stereo microscope)

rulers

construction paper

For any age level, I know I want space for children to work together. Minimally, this could mean two desks set side by side, with display space on top and clipboards handy for writing. Long tables are great—they allow enough space both to set up displays and to accommodate three to six children (Figure 2–3).

If possible, I put the table in a part of the room where it will be easily seen—along a wall in the middle of the room, or in a place that can be seen from the doorway. I want children to notice a new display right away or to be able to "check in" on the pollywogs as they head to math group, or clean up. It needs to be located where children can concentrate on observing, drawing, and writing, but not where extreme quiet is always required. I might keep it at some distance from drama or carpentry or reading group tables, but near art or an independent

Figure 2–3	The science area in a five- and six-year-old classroom; note display space for children's work.

reading or math area. In addition to table and chairs, a bulletin board is helpful for displaying finished work (the nearer the science table the better). Reference books need to be located on shelves or tables where children can get them quickly, without disrupting other groups (Figure 2–4). If books are handy, they'll be put to use. If they're too far away or hard to find, they won't be.

Windows can be wonderful if you're growing plants, deadly if you're keeping a tank of guppies. Animals need protection from direct sunlight, so find a way to block the windows if that's the only spot for a science table where you plan on having animals.

Storage space for supplies (crayons, hand lenses, and worksheets) is important. Finished work also needs a place; baskets, folders, canvas pockets, and drawers all work well. (For additional information on room arrangement, see Charney et al. 1984.)

Figure 2–4	A deep windowsill provides handy storage for reference books

I love microscopes and find that seven- or eight-years-old is a good age for introducing low-magnification microscopes (also called dissecting, or stereo, microscopes) (Figure 2–5). But a good microscope is an expensive piece of equipment, and an outstanding science program can be run without one. Sometimes enough inexpensive hand lenses can be purchased for each child to have one, or a collection of magnifying lenses can be stored at the science table for everyone's use.

Some children want rulers to use for drawing straight lines or measuring specimens. I make rulers available, but seldom require their use. Children can compare sizes in many ways:

"The green feather is bigger than the brown one."

"This rock is as big as my hand!" (We need to keep in mind, of course, that a child not yet conserving number, area, or volume may size things up quite differently than we do!) Until children can deal easily with the fractional amounts on a ruler, they may go through the motions of measuring, but their results may not be accurate. I want children to be comparing and thinking about size, but I don't want them to get too bogged down trying to figure out fractions. If knowing size is important to children (as it might be to a group studying birds and making frequent use of field guides where measurements are given),

Figure 2–5	Seven-or eight-years-old is a good age for introducing the stereomicroscope

then we work on it together: "Here is how you measure—wing tip to wing tip." Even then, all individuals do not have to be skilled at measuring for us to proceed. One child in a group might care to get out the ruler; a partner can contribute by describing and drawing the beak and comparing it to pictures.

Colored construction paper or poster board is a great help when making displays. Colors can be chosen to present objects attractively and to help them be more visible (black under sand or a light colored feather, white under a glass dish of water with pond animals). And when the space at the table is well defined (pencils in the can, shells arranged on the colored paper), children can keep the area neat and take good care of delicate specimens (Figure 2–6). Maintaining the science area—keeping it organized and beautiful—is worth the effort it takes. In setting up this area, we've said, "Science is important here." If we allow it to collect dust, become cluttered, or if specimens are frequently lost or damaged, we change our message to "Well— not *that* important!"

Figure 2–6	Colored construction paper helps present objects attractively and defines space so that students can take care of delicate specimens.

A: Display by student

B: Display by teacher of samples students collected on a field trip

Worksheets: Their Role in Classroom Science

Scientists of all ages keep records. I sometimes make use of notebooks and drawing paper for record keeping, and I often use worksheets. Why use worksheets when so many of us have hated the reams of dreadful dittos we were required to fill out? Good worksheets add to the definition of an activity (Figure 2–7). They indicate some ways of approaching it, some boundaries. This can help when children begin, especially if they are accustomed to lots of teacher-directed work requiring them to answer specific questions. Simply sending them off to observe can be too open-ended or vague for some children.

The worksheet can suggest a way to proceed without narrowing children's responses to that "one right answer." It can say, "Tell your

| Figure 2–7 | **Good worksheets add definition to an activity without narrowing responses to that "one right answer"** |

name and what you looked at. Draw what you see in this space. Notice some things and write about them here." I provide worksheets for children to use at the science table. Samples are included in the Appendix for duplication. Eventually, some children will be able to design their own worksheets.

When I organize a project for children, I search for a balance between direction and open-ended possibilities. I want to organize the work so that the children know what is expected and how to begin. I also want to provide enough freedom for the children to work in their own ways and trust their own ideas, priorities, and ways of proceeding. Worksheets can be designed that provide this balance. On the worksheets I use, children can begin by drawing or writing. They can write a little or a lot, draw a top view, side view, scale drawing, and so on. Like the science table and the observation activity, the worksheet provides just enough structure for children to feel in control, to know how to begin. Within that structure there is much freedom.

A certain amount of structure is freeing, and when children have outgrown the structure we have provided, they often show us. They may come to us and say:

"Can I add another sheet?"

"Can I use drawing paper instead?"

"Can I do a report?"

"I have an experiment I want to try."

Other times we may observe that something isn't working. For example, a group of seven- and eight-year-olds was studying birds; they were keenly interested in some nests that had been brought in. They'd had some success identifying birds and decided to identify the nests as well. It proved to be a frustrating task, and I noticed some children giving up and others quickly assigning a label (usually inaccurate).

Generally, interest in the nests seemed to be diminishing. I discussed the difficulty of this work with the class and designed a worksheet with a set of steps to help them approach the task of identification differently (Figure 2–8). Interest in the work was renewed, and the particular difficulty of nest identification was underlined when several adult "experts" the children consulted each assigned a different label to the same nest.

As children record their observations, I keep in mind that the finished product is just one aspect of their work. Product and process are interwoven. Drawing an object helps us see it, as well as show others what it is that we see. Products help us share and provide points of closure. But the ever continuing work and the activity and dialogue around the worksheet generate the excitement. If they are not cultivated, the worksheet will become just another ditto to be completed.

A worksheet need not be done each time children observe at the science table. Children may spend hours watching pond animals or guinea pigs for each sheet produced. Drawing and writing are de-

Worksheets: Their Role in Classroom Science

Figure 2–8	A worksheet designed to help children approach the difficult task of identifying bird nests

Composition of a Nest	Mystery Question:

The nest I observed is made of:

_____ mud

__V__ grasses

_____ twigs

_____ leaves

_____ roots

__V__ Other: FUZ

weeds

Description of the nest:
not that open
Spunge

The nest is approximately the size of: SoFet ball

Where was the nest found:
Rosberry Boosh

WHAT BIRD MADE THIS NEST?

5 Birds that could not have made this nest are: a Trumpeter swan, Beacus it is To big asterage Beacus it is to big a Hawk Beacus the nest is To small clif Swalowe Beacas Thar nest is much DiFrent Owl Beacas Thay Don't Live in Rasbbery Bushes

3 birds that might have made this nest are: BaLtamor oryeL beacus Thay Do NOT X nes Twigs The orckard oryeL Beacas The nest Looks the Same in a Field Gied Red Eyd viros

My hypothesis is that BaLtemor OraL beacus made this nest because: 1. it is a hanging it is nest 2. The Range is Right 3. it wold Fit in The nest

---

manding activities, and children need time free from this activity just to look. Requiring a product can help children look and share, but it can also get in the way. Again, I search for balance, so that ''Observe'' does not come to mean ''Fill out a worksheet.''

Before school opens, my time is spent structuring a classroom that will offer both freedom to explore and sufficient structure to generate learning. Careful organization of the physical environment invites children to participate in science activities. Once the room is ready, I turn my thoughts to how I shall introduce science to a new class of children.

3

The First Class Meeting: What Do Scientists Do?

When the children start school in September, I know I'll spend weeks working with them on how to use our room. Areas will be opened one by one, equipment and materials introduced carefully and deliberately. I open the science area right away, often during the first week of school. The first work we do involves observing an object, plant, or animal, and recording what is observed. Observing continues throughout the year, and the years. It's a process we focus on and develop, whether we're five or eleven (or thirty or fifty), and whether we're studying rocks or frogs, batteries or rivers. Before the children arrive, I give thought to a starting place. Sometimes I choose an object that relates to a topic we'll study in depth—a feather if it's birds, an apple if it's food. Other times it's an object apart from any theme or unit, something that intrigues me, that I think will interest children—something sturdy enough to be handled a bit—perhaps a beautiful shell, a bone, a flower. Certain things strike me as particularly interesting for different ages. For sevens—who love those tiny worlds—I might choose a cricket, or dragonfly, or colorful caterpillar; for fives and sixes—something familiar—a pet, a garden vegetable; for tens or elevens—something mysterious, or partly mysterious, so that a little looking and research will be required to discern its identity.

The First Meeting

The science area and science work are introduced to children during a meeting. It can involve a small group or the entire class. During this meeting, I try to find out what children already know about scientists

35

and about how we will work in our room. I generate with the children any rules we'll need for working. Where can kids work? When? With what? Can the guinea pig be held and patted, or do fingers stay out of the cage? Together we rehearse how we will work. I ask someone to demonstrate how to get paper and find a work place and have children practice looking closely, describing what they notice, looking again.

Meetings with Younger Children

The following example of a first science meeting is from a classroom of five- and six-year-olds. In this example I elected to work with a group of nine children, while the rest of the class worked independently in different areas of the room. The science group was seated in a circle on our meeting rug, not far from the science table. A large chart stand was situated where all of the children could see it.

Teacher: Today we're going to start some work that we'll be doing all year long. Today we're going to start our science work! What are the people who do science work called? They have a special name—what's that name?

Danny: Scientists.

Teacher: Scientists. Have you heard that word? (*I write ''Scientists'' on the chart*.) That's how the word looks. Scientists. Fancy word! Right now, you're going to turn into scientists. What is it that scientists do?

Laurie: They look at things.

Teacher: They look at things. Yes. (*I repeat Laurie's idea as I write it on the chart*.) What else do they do?

Rachel: They look at bugs . . .

Teacher (*again, writing*): They look at bugs.

Rachel: . . . and they see what kind they are.

Teacher (*noticing a child's hand*): You had an idea.

Neil: They discover things.

Teacher: They discover things. (*I nod to Alex*.)

Alex: They do paintings.

Teacher: They do paintings. What do you think a scientist might do a painting of?

Alex: Well, maybe sometimes they do weird paintings, like they go down and they go up, then that way, that way, then all around. (He demonstrates as he explains.)

Teacher: What would a scientist want to show people in a painting? Or what might a scientist make a painting of?

Rachel: They could make a painting of a bug.

Teacher: A scientist might make a painting of a bug to show other people what the bug looked like. Any other ideas?

Michael: Um, a horse.

Teacher: A scientist might make a painting of a horse, if he or she was studying horses.

Teacher: Yes. Are there any other kinds of jobs they do? (*I point to our list.*) They might look at things, they might discover things, paint what they see. Do they do any other kinds of work?

Neil: Um, they might dig up dinosaur bones.

Teacher: They might! Have you ever heard of a scientist digging up dinosaur bones?

Neil: Yes, I seen a movie of it.

Teacher: And you thought of something else.

Neil: They might fit them together.

Teacher: They might fit them together.

Brian: And I saw a real skeleton.

Teacher: They might fit all the bones together and have a skeleton! Can you think of something else, Kathleen, that a scientist would do?

Kathleen: They study gold.

Teacher: They might study gold. I'm ready for three more ideas of things you think a scientist would do.

Danny: They might if they put some more pieces of dinosaur bones together. They might know where things go and then they would make a model.

Teacher: So they'd make a model—try and figure out how everything went together. Michael? Did you have a different idea?

Michael: I forgot.

Teacher: Timmy?

Timmy: I know what scientists do! They look for Indian stuff.

Teacher (*looking over list*): Here's our list. We figured out all these things that scientists do. We think that scientists are people

    who look at things;

    who look at bugs;

    who discover things;

    who do paintings, maybe of a bug or a horse;

who sometimes dig up dinosaur bones and fit them together and then make a model;

who sometimes study gold; or

who look for Indian stuff.

Well, right now, you're going to do some science work, and here's where we're going to start—we'll start with this one: "Scientists look at things." (*I underline this idea on the chart as I read it aloud.*) When scientists look at things, they have a very special name for what they're doing. Do you know what it is?

Several children: No. (*A few others shake their heads.*)

Teacher: They don't say, "Hey, let's go look at stuff," they . . .

Brian: They make discoveries.

Teacher: Yes! And here's the thing they have to do to make discoveries. It's a big word. I'm going to write it up here. Then I'm going to say it. "Observe." Did you ever hear that word? What does it mean?

Timmy: You could put that in a box.

Teacher: Okay. I'll put it in a box. (*I draw a box around the word.*) There it is. "Observe." It's a fancy word for doing what?

Neil: Looking at things.

Teacher: It means look at things. How do you think a scientist would look at things? "Observe" means you look, and how do you look?

Rachel: Carefully.

Teacher: You look really carefully. And that's part of how you can make a discovery. Make a big space in the middle of this circle. I'm going to bring you something to observe.

Rachel (*motioning as she slides back on the floor*): This far . . . we have to back up! (*I return to the group, carrying a large animal cage.*)

Several children: The guinea pig.

Michael: The second time I've seen it!

Danny (*to his neighbor*): I knew it.

Teacher: Here it is. (*I place the cage in the middle of the circle and sit down. I won't be writing during this part of the meeting.*) Looks like Neil is getting kind of crowded out. How can we fix this circle so everyone can see? (*Kathleen wiggles back on the floor.*) Good idea, Kathleen.

Right now it's your time to observe our guinea pig. You already know how to hold this guinea pig, and pat and feed him. This time, you're going to observe him. And what does that mean?

Neil: Study him.

Teacher: Yes, study him . . . by doing what?

Timmy: Marking him.

Teacher: Are we going to mark him?

Timmy: No.

Teacher: What did we say we're going to do?

Alex and Rachel: Look at him!

Teacher: Right. Rachel, when you observe this guinea pig, when you look at him really carefully, what's something that you notice about him? What's something you can see?

Rachel: He has teeth.

Teacher: He has teeth. Is that the kind of thing a scientist would notice?

Rachel: Yes.

Teacher: You bet. What do you notice when you observe him, Timmy?

Timmy: He drinks and he eats.

Teacher: He drinks and he eats. We've seen that before! Is that what he's doing right now?

Timmy: No.

Teacher: What's something he's doing right now?

Timmy: Walking around.

Teacher: Timmy noticed him walking around. Brian, what can you see from looking at our guinea pig?

Brian: He's furry.

Teacher: He's furry. Would a scientist notice if an animal has fur?

Brian: Yes.

Teacher (*nodding in agreement*): You bet! Michael, what's something you notice?

Michael: I don't know.

Teacher: Well, take a look at him. Is there something you notice when you look really carefully?

Michael: He nibbles at the cage.

Teacher: He nibbles at the cage. And what do you notice?

Alex: I can see through his ears and it's dark in his ears.

Teacher: You can see through his ears and it's dark in his ears. You were really looking carefully if you noticed that!

Teacher: What do you notice, Laurie?

Laurie: His ears.

Teacher: What do you notice about those ears?

Laurie: They're little.

Teacher: This guinea pig has little ears, not great big rabbit ears. (*Timmy laughs.*)

Teacher: A scientist would have to pay attention to that. How come? (*There is no response. I realize these children have a beginning understanding of what scientists do. This question demands an ability to generalize that is beyond their age and experience. So I try again.*) Are all animals just the same, with the same kind of ears?

Children (*laughing*): No!

Teacher: No—so scientists have to look very carefully. (*The guinea pig squeaks.*)

Laurie (*giggling*): Funny!

Teacher: What did you notice right now?

Timmy: He took a squeak.

Teacher: Did you notice that from looking at him?

Children: No.

Teacher: How?

Laurie: From hearing him.

Teacher: So sometimes when scientists observe, they listen. (*Rachel looks like she wants to say something.*) Do you have another thing, Rachel?

Rachel: There's a log in his cage.

Teacher: Yes. Randy put that in for him to chew on. Neil, did you notice one more thing?

Neil: He stood up!

Teacher: Our guinea pig can stand up.

Michael: He has whiskers.

Teacher: What are you noticing, Kathleen?

Kathleen: He scratches.

Teacher: Right now you're going to do an observation of this guinea pig, and you've been working on it already. You've been looking and listening and noticing and telling me lots of things you've noticed. But you know what? There's a special way for you to keep track of all the things you notice about our guinea pig. Laurie, I want you to stand up and walk over to the science table. Show everyone where we keep the observation sheets we use for keeping track. (*Laurie crosses to the science table, and locates a cardboard pocket on the bulletin board.*) Great.

Now count out one for each person. (*While she is counting, I turn to the group*.) How many do you think she'll need? Nine, that's a lot!

Laurie (*returning with a stack of worksheets*): I don't know if it's the right number.

Teacher (*I nod reassurance*): Now, Laurie brought you these. This is a special paper that you're going to work on when you do your science observation. Look what it has on it. Up at the top it says, "Name of Scientist". If this were Rachel's paper, what would go here?

Children: "Rachel."

Teacher: If this were Neil's paper, what would go here?

Children: "Neil."

Teacher: And here it says, "I looked at" and there's a long line. What am I looking at?

Children: The guinea pig.

Teacher: For today, if you want to write "guinea pig", you may. You don't have to, but you may if you wish. In this big box it says, "A picture of what I saw." What will you make a careful drawing of in here?

Rachel: Guinea pig.

Teacher: You'll draw just how he looks to you. Will you draw him with a big long tail and a hard shell?

Children: No!

Teacher: How come, Timmy?

Timmy: Because he doesn't have any tail.

Teacher: What does he have? What will you give him?

Timmy: Fur, fur, fur, fur.

Teacher: Lots of fur. Down at the bottom, if you're the kind of scientist who'd like to do some writing, it says, "I noticed" and there's room for you to write. What's something you could write that you noticed?

Timmy: His ears are little.

Teacher: Okay. I think you're ready. What will you do your drawing and writing with? What do you think would be good things for a scientist to use?

Danny: Pencils.

Teacher: Yes. And if you want to show color, what will help?

Children: Markers, crayons, colored pencils.

Teacher: Markers write so dark, we'll just use them once in a while.

But crayons and pencils we'll use a lot! If you look over at the science table, you'll see where we keep the crayons and pencils that you can use. You'll also see a pocket for work that is finished.

(*I move to the periphery of the group. Now is the time for the children to observe the guinea pig, and for me to observe the children.*) (Figure 3–1)

Generally, the children's ideas at five about what scientists do will be fairly literal and specific. They may confuse science with other professions, get involved listing many examples of a particular activity, or relate personal stories. Teachers can gauge how much of this is productive. For five-year-olds, this first science meeting (like all meetings) needs to be kept quite short. Ten minutes is sufficient time to collect ideas about what scientists do and what the children will do in their work as scientists (including caring for materials). There will be many more meetings, and you can add to your list.

Meetings with Older Children

At six, seven, eight, and even older, the basic format of this initial meeting is essentially the same. Of course, children bring something different to their work each year—new understanding, abilities, and experience. The evolution of responses to "what do scientists do" can be seen in this example from a six-year-old: "Well, scientists don't really know everything, which most people think they do, but they don't. What they do is they try to figure out a lot of things, because people think that scientists know everything but they don't. They're trying to know a lot, so they get other scientists to help them, and also usually people figure things out by making mistakes."

A classmate contributed: "They study insects by spying on them in the woods. Well, they don't really spy. They just go in the woods and look around and see what they can figure out about the insects by looking at them. And then they bring them back into their laboratory and study them."

"What's a laboratory?" inquired the teacher.

"Oh, it's a place where the scientists do all their creations and they study with their microscopes."

Another six-year-old added: "Sometimes scientists might have labs bigger than the school because they have tons of things in there and they stay up all night to figure out stuff."

| Figure 3–1 | The children record their observations of the class's guinea pig |

A: Guinea pig by Timmy, age five

B: Guinea pig by Neil, age five

C: Guinea pig by Laurie, age five

A group of seven- and eight-year-olds came up with the following list of what scientists do:

study one thing or many

do research

make pictures of what they see

write reports in books

write down what they notice

watch birds

take care of living things

take care of themselves

go up in trees

observe

look at things

take notes

do fieldwork

At this age some answers are quite specific, others more general. An awareness of a wide range of scientific activities is reflected here.

With sevens, eights, and older children, I may start to explore the idea of objectivity. With fives and sixes, this idea comes up, but the egocentrism of young children means we'll only get so far, as was the case with Katie, a five-year-old. Cuddling the guinea pig in her lap, Katie exclaimed, eyes sparkling, "He likes me!" When I asked her how she could tell, she answered, "'Cause look how he's staying right here. That means he likes me."

Older children are generally aware of many aspects of scientific work and are ready to consider more questions and possibilities than younger children. Ruthie, almost eight, demonstrated this while watching the chicks we had hatched. As she put her hand down into the box, a chick scrambled over and pecked at her silver ring.

"Look! He likes me!" she giggled.

"How can you tell?" I asked.

"Well, he ran over and started pecking when I put my hand in."

"Do you think these chicks have feelings about people, the way we do about our friends? They like them or they don't like them?"

"Well . . . maybe."

"Scientists are interested in what animals think, but it is hard to find out about it. We can't ask them!"

Ruthie laughed, "No, we can't!"

"But what just happened was exciting and interesting for you," I pointed out. "So how can you tell other scientists about what just happened?"

"Well, I could say that when I put my hand in the box, this chick ran over and pecked me."

"Yes, I saw that happen. And how could you talk about your idea that he likes you?"

"I could say, maybe he likes me, or I could try to find out more about it."

With older children, the first class meeting may include a discussion of the kind of language scientists use when reporting observations and the need for clarity and accuracy, as in this meeting with seven- and eight-year-olds.

Teacher: How about if I write that it's really old? (*I am holding up a large bone.*)

Jenny: Well, it does *look* old.

Teacher: What makes you think so?

Jenny: Those holes, and the way it's sort of worn on one end.

Chris: And smooth on top.

Teacher: So, shall I write "it's old"? Is that something I've observed?

Nancy: It could just be damaged, but not really that old.

Teacher: Scientists are very careful with their words. They don't want people to be confused! So what words would tell what I see about this bone?

Mark: You could say that it has holes, and it's smooth in places.

Teacher: And if I want to keep track of my idea that it's old, how can I say that in a way everyone would be clear about what I mean?

Melissa: You could say, "I think it's old."

Emily: Or "it looks old."

I want to make it clear, at this point, how I understand objectivity. One may try, in science, to observe the world around without feelings, prior knowledge, or prejudices distorting one's perceptions, but in fact, these separations are not entirely possible. We are not detached observers of our world, reporting facts and truths that are quite separate from ourselves. We construct what we know, and we may have an impact on what we observe.

I find that an exaggerated emphasis on "fact vs. opinion," "correct vs. incorrect," or a particular standard for objectivity confuses children about the aims and possibilities of science, and distracts us from the business of observing, thinking about, and discussing our surroundings. Instead, I encourage children to become aware of assumptions and biases, to compare observations with knowledge acquired in other ways, and to compare one observation with another. We also work to find language that expresses our experience as clearly as possible. The following example from a group of nine-, ten-, and eleven-year-old girls provides further illustration of this and also shows how older children respond at a first meeting. Note that the format is basically the same as with five- and six-year-olds, but the children's responses reflect their increased age and experience.

Teacher: Today, we're going to start our science work. What is it that scientists do?

Beth: Well, they do research on stuff. And there's different kinds of scientists.

Teacher (*nodding*): There are.

Beth: Lots of different kinds!

Teacher: What are some?

Beth: I don't know—like—entomologists.

Teacher: Entomologists. That's quite a word! What do entomologists do?

Beth: Um, I forget, but . . .

Teacher: But some of you have heard that word? It is a word for a special kind of scientist.

Debbie: I forget what they're called, but there's a kind of scientist that studies bugs.

Teacher: That's it! Entomologists study insects.

Debbie: They have a different name.

Teacher: Hmm. We had a different name last year for the scientists that study birds. Anybody remember that one? (*A few head shakes, some blank looks*).

Teacher: Here's how it looks (*I write on chart:* ''ornithologists'').

Debbie: Oh, yes!

Teacher: Okay. Beth says that there's lots of different kinds of scientists, and that they do research. What do you mean, ''research?''

Beth: Research about what, you know . . .

Liz: The things they study.

Terry: Like if they're an entomologist, they do research on bugs.

Teacher: Other ideas about what scientists do?

Debbie: Their research is trying to figure out more about the subject that they're studying.

Teacher: Yes! That's a good way to put it (*I write* ''Research— trying to figure out more about the subject''). So things like insects are examples of . . .

Debbie: What they're studying.

Teacher: Any other ideas about what scientists do?

Susan: There's a group of scientists that are on TV a lot. They're studying birds that are extinct, that are getting extinct. And they're trying to find ways to help them. Like they're feeding them with puppets that look like what their mothers look like.

Teacher: So some scientists are not only studying about something, and trying to find out more about a subject, they're actually trying to change something, or do something.

Susan: The California condors. They're working on breeding them. They're taking the eggs so the parents will lay more.

Teacher: That's right. Scientists are trying to keep condors from becoming extinct. I'm going to use this word "prevent" (*I write* "prevent"). You've probably heard "prevent tooth decay." Well, "prevent extinction" means . . .

Marjie: Keep it from happening.

Teacher: What does "extinct" mean?

Susan: That there's no more left, like dinosaurs.

Teacher: Are there other things you know about that scientists do? Joan?

Joan: Study the ocean.

Teacher (*I repeat answer while writing*): Study the ocean.

Lisa: Marine biologists!

Teacher: Yes, they might be marine biologists, or oceanographers.

Liz: Some scientists study rocks.

Teacher: Yes, they do, and they have a special name, too. Does anybody know it?

Susan: Rocktologists?

Teacher: Rocktologists would be good, but that's not the one they use. Scientists who study rocks are called "geologists."

During the next few minutes, children generated the names of many different scientific specialties. When we had identified most of the major categories, we began to discuss how scientists work.

Teacher: All of these different kinds of scientists that you thought of have some things in common. Debbie said they have different subjects they study. Some study the stars; some study insects; some work on the problem of air pollution. They have different specialities, but they have some things in common as well. Beth said at the beginning of our meeting that one thing they have in common is they do research.

Susan: And they study.

Teacher: They all have something that they study, yes. Is there anything else you can think of that all scientists have in common?

Debbie: They all have the name "Scientist"!

Beth: They all have "ogist" at the end of their names.

Teacher: They do! What else do we know? We know that scientists do research. Do they do anything else?

Susan: Well, they're working to try and find out more about something. So they can help prevent it, or make it better. They have different reasons they want to find out, but in their research they're all trying to find out more about something.

Teacher: What are the things that they do to find out? Jennifer, can you think of one?

Jennifer: Well, if they wanted to find out more about a certain kind of bird, they'd watch it.

Teacher: They'd watch it.

Kathy: They'd do tests.

Teacher: They'd do tests. The kind where you have to spell a word right?

Kathy: No! The kind where you have to do different tests on the subject, um, like . . .

Teacher: It's a hard thing to describe.

Kathy: Like designing a test to figure out more.

Lisa: Observations.

Susan: A scientist was trying to find out how poisonous a certain kind of fish was so she put a plastic bag over some coral. Pretty soon all the other fish in the bag were dead from the poison. (*Unlike the five- and six-year-olds, Susan can relate cause and effect, and is aware that scientists sometimes manipulate the world in order to answer a question.*)

Teacher: Wow! What do you call the thing she did to find out?

Susan: A test.

Teacher: It's a test. And there's another word for it, too.

Marjie: Experiment.

Teacher: Experiment. Debbie, did you have one more idea?

Debbie: I did. But now I forgot.

Teacher: Well, when you think of it you let me know. So, scientists have different subjects that they study. But they're all trying to find out more about the things that they care about by watching, observing, doing tests, and experimenting.

Debbie: Well, they do have special places where they work. Like sanctuaries, where one kind of bird is. And so they set up lines, so if they want to learn more about the mating habits they can.

Teacher: So sometimes there is a special place where scientists do their work. You are going to start your own work right now, in this special place. You're going to start by doing an observation. Lisa brought up that word a minute ago, and it's related to one Jennifer brought up earlier—"watch" (*I point it out on chart*).

Teacher: When you observe, what is it that you do?

Jennifer: You watch them.

Liz: You draw what you see.

Teacher: Yes. And today you get to watch.

Children: Checkers! (*I bring out the class guinea pig.*)

Teacher: Now I know that some of you have already spent a *lot* of time with Checkers! For instance, I know that Beth has noticed lots of things about him. (*Beth nods vigorously.*)

Teacher: What's something you notice when you observe him right now?

Debbie: His hair looks coarse.

Teacher: Coarse-looking hair.

Susan: He squeaks a lot.

Teacher: A lot!

Teacher: I notice Debbie did something. She was very careful about the words she used to report her observation. Debbie said that this guinea pig's fur *looks* coarse. Scientists need to be very careful with their words. How come?

Beth: Well, Debbie said it looks coarse.

Debbie: I don't *know.*

Susan: She didn't touch it yet so she doesn't know for sure. (*The children laugh as the guinea pig chews on the bars of his cage and squeaks.*)

Marjie: He chews his bars!

Beth: His eyes are red.

Teacher: What would happen if scientists weren't so careful with their words? If Debbie said his hair *is* coarse?

Susan: Well, if it was soft, then she'd say something she didn't really mean.

Teacher: That's right. So scientists are trying to report just what they did notice.

Debbie (*laughing*): He looks like a dog!

Teacher: What can you see when he does all that funny chewing?

Liz: He doesn't use his teeth.

Teacher: What are his teeth like? Can you get a good look at them?

Beth: The front teeth are *very* big! (*She demonstrates.*)

Susan: They're like beaver's teeth.

Teacher (*nodding*): Like beaver's teeth.

Beth: Something I noticed a long time ago is they have four toes on the front feet and three on the back.

Teacher: Do you want to show people that? (*Beth shows the guinea pig around.*)

Teacher: What about us? What do we have?

Joan: Same—five fingers, five toes.

Teacher: What about some other animals, like dogs?

Several girls: I don't know.

Joan: The same, I think.

Debbie: Haven't they got four?

Lisa: But some dogs have a little toe, a dew claw.

Teacher: Yes. I was surprised when I first noticed the guinea pig's toes. I had just assumed there would be the same number, front and back. Debbie talked before about his fur. Would anyone like the chance to hold him for a minute to see how he feels? (*Children nod.*)

Beth (*picking up the guinea pig*): He feels soft! Kathy's turn.

Kathy: I can't hold him.

Teacher: That's right! In fact we'll want to keep him a good distance from Kathy when we take our turns. Being close to a guinea pig won't help her allergies any! Time to pass him on to Jennifer. Right now there's time for just a quick turn each, but later this afternoon there will be time for more. What are some things you're noticing?

Liz (*laughing*): He's chewing on Jennifer's hair!

Teacher: Chewing on her hair!

Debbie: He's curious.

Teacher: Curious. What do you see that makes you think so? (*I want them to begin to distinguish between their observations and inferences.*)

Debbie: He's sniffing around.

Susan: And squeaking.

Beth: I noticed this about mine: when you pet her in different places she makes different kinds of squeaks.

Teacher: Really?

Beth: Like when you pet her down her back she goes "purrrr" but when you touch her around the neck she goes "weak weak weak weak."

Teacher: So she makes different sounds in different kinds of situations.

Susan: This guinea pig is squeaking like mad!

Teacher: I wonder if it is disturbing to him to be passed around a circle of giants? I notice how gently you are touching him, and how still you are sitting. You're doing what you can to make this meeting safe for him.

Liz: My rabbit was that size when I got her.

Teacher: Little! While the last turns are being taken, you can get to work on your own observations. Remember these worksheets?

Children: Yes.

Teacher: Here's a place for . . .

Beth: Name and date.

Joan: And what you're observing.

Teacher: What materials do you need to get to help with this work?

Girls: Clipboards. Pencils. We have colored pencils, too.

Teacher: Great! I'm going to slide his cage out into the middle of the circle so you can see him from all sides (Figure 3–2).

During the first class meeting I elicit from the children what they know about what scientists do. Together we define and practice one aspect of this work. Over the course of the year, I'll hope to see children involved in all kinds of science activity (collecting, classifying, hypothesizing, experimenting), but initially I emphasize observation. A look at the previous examples reveals children observing, but also

Figure 3–2	Guinea pig by ten-year-old girl

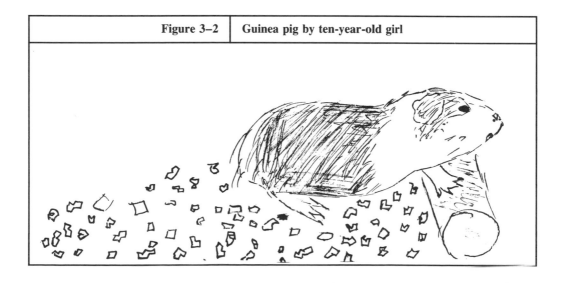

sharing information and ideas, interpreting their observations, identifying patterns, reacting to things that seem funny or surprising, and
drawing on information from previous experiences. Just as scientists
employ many skills simultaneously, children can make use of more
than one ability at a time. Observation serves as the springboard for
children to engage in work that is far broader in scope than simply
looking at an object.

Children's First Work Period

After the first meeting, children need an opportunity to observe something themselves, either during a work period immediately following the meeting, or later on that day. If they won't have an opportunity to observe until later in the week, children will do best with five minutes of reviewing how a scientist works before they begin.

I plan to be available to children during their first observation session so that I can observe their different working styles, ask questions, and reinforce the positive behavior I see. I'm also there to reassure children who feel unsure of what to do and give reminders, if they are needed, about ways to handle animals and materials. Although I prepare a place for finished work, I know some children will need to "check in" before proceeding with each new step ("Is this where I put my paper?"), and many children will want to share their first observations before handing them in.

As children begin to work, I am aware that I need to make careful decisions about what I do and say. My thoughts return to our meeting. The children have told me what scientists do. Together we have defined observation as looking carefully, listening, touching, and noticing. We have also established some guidelines for working: we'll use worksheets and crayons and pencils; we'll draw and maybe write; we'll keep pencils and fingers out of the guinea pig's cage. These are the behaviors I'm expecting to see, and I identify them out loud when I do:

"I see you remembered where we keep the observation sheets, Danny."

"I notice you found a brown crayon to show the color of this guinea pig's fur, Alex."

"I see you looking so carefully, Laurie. That's just what scientists do."

Of course, I'm also expecting some other behaviors. Someone will have trouble getting settled; another child will be hesitant to begin drawing; two children will want the same brown crayon. I search for simple and positive ways to help children remember their jobs and begin working:

"Where will you sit to do your work, Margaret? Is there a space you can see that looks like a good place to observe this guinea pig from?"

"What do you notice when you look at this guinea pig, Neil? Is that something you could put in your drawing?"

"Two scientists noticed brown fur and are ready to draw it! What do you need so that you both can work?"

The following describes the first observation of our guinea pig by a group of five-year-olds. We had already met to define observation and discuss how we would work. Now nine children were ready to begin. Since our science table could comfortably seat just three children, I needed to make some special provisions:

"Nine scientists will be working together, so we can't all fit at the science table. We'll stay here to do our work today. Laurie and Michael, you can get crayons for us. Neil and Timmy, you can go get your observation sheets and a clipboard from the shelf. Rachel and Brian, now it's your turn."

As children returned with their materials, I moved to the periphery of the circle and watched. I noticed how quickly Brian settled down to work—looking at the guinea pig, drawing, looking again. Laurie had a selection of crayons spread out in front of her. She was working on her name—each letter a different, beautiful color. Neil held a clipboard, paper, and pencil as he watched two children in the block area. He continued to stand, but shifted his gaze to the guinea pig and the other children at work. Alex looked up at me.

Alex: Does it go this way? (*I nod.*) Is here where I put my name? (*I nod again.*) What does this say?

Teacher: "A picture of what I saw." (*I notice Timmy, sitting cross-legged, very close to one corner of the guinea pig cage. Tap tap tap goes his pencil on the edge of his clipboard.*) I see you found all the things you need to start your observation. (*I move about the group of children a bit.*) I see you keep looking again and again at that guiniea pig, Brian. You are drawing the things you notice about him. I see you really studying that guinea pig, Rachel. You remembered where to put your picture on this sheet, Alex. (*After a few minutes, Rachel brings me her paper.*)

Rachel: I messed up!

Teacher: Show me.

Rachel (*pointing to a circular shape she has drawn*): There. (*Together, we look at her paper.*)

Teacher: You don't like this part?

Rachel: No.

Teacher: How do you want it to be?

Rachel (*pointing to her work*): His head, here.

Teacher (*I consider a moment*): Well, a guinea pig is a hard thing to draw, and you have noticed lots of things you want to show in your picture! Do you want to try again over here (*I point to space near her first try*) or get another sheet?

Rachel: Get another sheet.

Teacher: Fine. (*After just five minutes of work, Danny is at my side.*)

Danny: I'm done (*tosses his paper my way*).

Teacher: Come tell me about this work! I see brown here—the color of his fur. And you noticed some things here. (*I point to the head end of his guinea pig.*)

Danny: His eyes and ears and nose.

Teacher: You noticed all those parts! I'm going to take a look at those eyes. (*I move closer to the cage.*) Did you get a look at the color of his eyes?

Danny: Looks black.

Teacher: Black eyes. Not like yours! Yours are blue! How would you show the color of his eyes in your drawing? (*Danny holds up a black crayon.*) That would really show people what you noticed. (*I figure Danny will color in the eyes and be done again. Maybe I'll have him just sit with the group and watch the guinea pig and talk, or maybe have him join another group of children somewhere else in the room. I notice Kathleen playing with her bracelet.*)

Teacher: How is your work going?

Kathleen: I don't want to observe the guinea pig. It's boring!

Teacher: The guinea pig is boring for you.

Kathleen: I already know about guinea pigs!

Teacher: You do! Do you have one at home?

Kathleen: No. At my old nursery school.

Teacher: So you know about some of the things they do! (*Kathleen nods and rolls her eyes.*)

Teacher (*addressing the whole group*): Did you know that some scientists just study one kind of animal? They watch one kind of animal, and they learn about what it does. They get so interested, they keep watching and they find out even more.

Every day they keep observing the same thing. They really stay interested. They get to be experts on one special kind of animal. Have you ever heard of that kind of scientist?

Kathleen: Yes! Diane . . . Diane, there's a movie about her.

Teacher: That's right! And she was an expert on . . .

Kathleen: Gorillas!

Teacher: Sometimes I have to help myself get interested. When I sit way back here, I can't see so well. This guinea pig doesn't seem so interesting. But when I get close (*I demonstrate by moving in*), then I start noticing things. Just look at what his nose is doing!
(*A few children look and giggle.*)

Children: Wiggling!

Teacher: Then I start wondering about that. (*I move off—leaving my bored child—uncertain whether she will need more help.*) Michael, I see you've figured out a way to show the shape of that guinea pig. You made a pointy face, and a flat back. Rachel! I can tell from your drawing you've been noticing the toes on this guinea pig! Could you tell how many he has?

Rachel: No.

Teacher: Do you want me to pick him up so you can see? (*Rachel nods and as I hold the guinea pig up, a number of children stop their work to watch.*)

Rachel (*counting the toes on his back feet first*): One, two, three.

Teacher: Three on the back. How about the front?

Rachel: One, two, three, four.
(*Some children look surprised.*)

Teacher: There are four toes on the front but three on the back. (*I put the guinea pig back in the cage. Rachel starts to erase some toes on her drawing. I notice that Timmy's tapping pencil is getting closer and closer to the cage.*) Timmy, if your finger or your pencil goes in his cage, what could happen?

Timmy: He could bite.

Teacher: Ouch! And it could also be scary for him. So fingers and pencils stay where?

Timmy: Out.

Teacher: Yes. You remember!

After about ten minutes, some children began to bring me their finished work. I held a very short conference with each. My pattern of responses ran along these lines: ''I see you showed the color of the guinea pig's fur''; ''Tell me something you noticed.'' I said something

Figure 4–1	Child (age six) with guinea pig

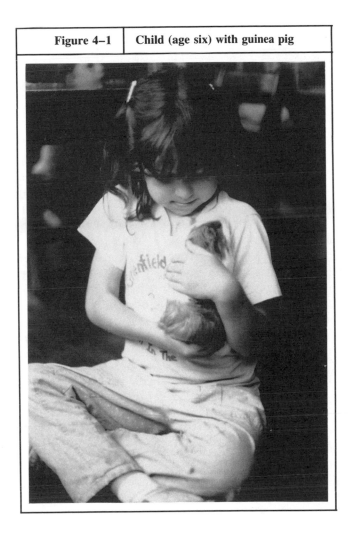

I had noticed about their drawing or how they had worked, and gave them each a chance to share an observation.

Then I offered a choice: "You can stay here and look at the guinea pig some more, and when everyone's through, we can have turns holding him, or you can choose another area in the room to work in." I wanted kids to enjoy learning about this animal (Figure 4–1). I wanted them to be able to take time learning about him in different ways and sharing with each other. I knew some children had already stayed with this activity as long as their attention spans would allow, but I didn't want to give the message that once the worksheet was completed there was nothing else to do.

The Teacher's Role During the First Work Period

During the first working period, the teacher's availability is especially important. If the entire class is doing a first observation at the same time, I circulate throughout the room. (I have often started the year this way with sevens and eights. I gather enough of the same type of object so that children can work in small groups of two to four. The initial meeting is a whole-class meeting; then we get immediately to work.) If, as in the previous example, part of the class is working on science, I plan to be free to work with that group. Of course, I'll keep an eye on the rest of the room, but I need to be able to devote most of my attention to the scientists.

In the previous example from the five-year-old room, I was quite free from certain duties often associated with teaching science. I was not lecturing or explaining. I was not telling children about the habits or life cycle of guinea pigs. Nor was I correcting work or presenting solutions to problems.

I was, however, very active. In trying to create a climate in which children would become active explorers of the world around them, in which both self-reliance and cooperation would be valued, I worked with deliberation.

I watched as children got settled at their work. I noticed Brian got to work quickly, focused on his observation. And I noticed Neil standing nearby, watching the blocks first, then the other children in his group. I expected that the children would work differently, and I watched to see what this behavior of Neil's meant. Was he wasting time? Doing nothing? Was he distracted or forgetful? Was he learning how to do an observation by watching others work, gaining the confidence he needed to make a try of his own? I heard Alex ask for reassurance before he began: "Does it go this way? Is here where I put my name?" He wanted to do this work right! By providing the reassurance he needed, I released him to make a start. Rachel also wanted her work to be good and right. At five and a half, visual confusions make drawing the guinea pig—and even writing her name—a difficult task. I thought she would feel best about her work if she could solve the problems she had defined, so I needed to help her with that definition, and support her as she attempted a solution. I was tempted to say, "This drawing is just fine!" or "Draw the head over here," but I knew these statements wouldn't help just then. Sometimes I was puzzled by what I saw, unsure of how to proceed. Kathleen told me she was bored. What did that mean? Was this work too familiar, and therefore uninteresting? Was the work too new, and therefore too threatening? Was she testing me, or was she a child who needed help to focus and become interested? I was not so sure. My intuition steered me toward one response. I might need to try again. And perhaps again.

My focus is very broad. I am as interested in the way these children are working as in the particular discoveries they make. In science, as in other areas of the curriculum, I need to pay attention to many things—the ways different children work, the kind of help each needs, and the discoveries each makes and records. I am not worried about giving the children lots of information about the guinea pig. In fact, I am quite excited about the content of this study, and I hope that the children will be. We have discovered many things about this guinea pig—that he squeaks and stands and wiggles his nose, that he has more toes on his front feet than on his back. His front teeth are long! And his ears are different colors. But this content is not something for me to discover and then place inside the children. Each will construct his or her own knowledge.

The kind of interaction between teacher and children seen in a five-year-old room is typical in classes with older children as well. In this example, I am working with the same group of nine- to eleven-year-old girls who began their science work in the previous chapter.

Teacher: I'm going to slide the guinea pig cage right out into the middle of the rug so you can see him from all sides. (*Girls get settled with clipboards, pencils, and observation sheets. Several begin drawing immediately, looking frequently from guinea pig to paper. Others watch the guinea pig. Susan notices his water bottle is low and removes it from the cage.*)

Debbie: I wish he would stay still! -

Teacher: You know, this is a trouble that scientists have when they try to draw animals. As soon as you get all settled to record what the animals are doing, they start doing something else! Some scientists get good at taking quick notes about the animal's behavior and making quick sketches.

Debbie: It's eating the cage again!

Teacher: You get a really good look at the mouth when he does that.

Lisa (*erasing her third start on a drawing*): Guinea pigs are hard to draw!

Beth (*pointing to her drawing*): I found an easy way. It's like they're sort of a shape—like a spread-out shape.

Teacher: So when you start to draw, Beth, you try to get the body shape first.

Beth: Then add the ears and all.

Teacher (*to Lisa*): You've got the curved shape of his back now. (*While the others have been drawing, Susan has been refilling the water bottle. She brings it back to the cage.*)

Susan (*indicating the bottle*): It's all green in there!

Beth: That happens to mine. I scrub it out with a toothbrush. (*The guinea pig begins squeaking loudly.*)

Liz: He's thirsty.

Teacher: He can't wait for Susan to put his bottle back!
(*Susan replaces the bottle and the guinea pig immediately begins drinking.*)

Teacher (*noticing Lisa's frustration*): Well, Lisa, I guess this guinea pig isn't going to make himself any easier to draw, standing up and lying down like that.

Jennifer: His feet—they look a lot like hands.

Teacher: Umhmm. What about them makes them look like that?

Jennifer: Well, like . . .

Liz: Fingers.

Jennifer: Yes, but . . . (*She shrugs, seems unable to explain.*)

Teacher: Try to show it in your picture.

Beth: On the bottom they look like hands; there are little pads, and they're fat.

Liz: They don't have a thumb.

Teacher: No, so they can't go like this (*I grab*) but they can go—how?
(*Jennifer shows by bending her fingers and clawing the air.*)

Beth: Their nose is sort of like . . . (*wiggles her own.*)

Teacher: You know, some of the things we've been saying, like when I said, "Checkers can't wait for Susan to put his bottle back," is that the kind of thing a scientist would write down as an observation?

Debbie: Not really.

Teacher: Why not?

Debbie: Well, they'd use more distinguished words.

Teacher: "Checkers can't wait" doesn't sound distinguished? Is anything else the matter?

Susan: Well, you're saying that he's definitely thirsty.

Teacher: It sounds like I might be saying that. Listen again. I said, "Checkers can't wait to get his bottle back." Is that what I observed?

Susan: You *think* he can't wait.

Teacher: Yes. And what did I see that gave me that idea?

Susan: Well, he was jumping around where the water bottle is. Then he started drinking.

Teacher: So if I don't want to confuse anybody, what's the clearest way for me to report?

Susan: It looks like he can't wait.

Teacher: Looks like. And what was the actual observation that I made?

Susan: He was jumping around.

Beth: Guinea pigs' eyes are really red.

Teacher: Red?

Beth: Now they look black, but if you see them in the light—then they're really red.

Teacher: So it depends on the light, how they look?

Beth: Yeah. I read about them in a book. Now they look black, but in the light, they're red.

Teacher: Their eyes are really red, but you can't see it. (*Off and on while the children observe and talk, the guinea pig returns to drink from his bottle.*)

Beth: He's still drinking! Look at his mouth!

Teacher: That would be hard to describe. How would you talk about it?

Beth: He sticks his tongue up in there and kind of pulls the water down.

Debbie: No, he pushes on the ball.

Teacher: What can you see him doing with his jaw when he drinks?

Girls: Biting.

Lisa: I can't make the legs!

Teacher: The legs are hard to draw.

Debbie: Very. I can never get proportions right.

Teacher: And a guinea pig has kind of unusual proportions How long are his legs?

Debbie: Very short compared to his body. At least it looks like that. But you know, a rabbit's tail just looks like a little puff. But if you stretch it all the way out, it's this long (*holds up thumb and finger to show*).

Kathy: Does he have a tail?

Beth: No.

Teacher: Do you want to see? I know you can't touch him, but if Beth holds him up you'll be able to get a good look. (*All of the girls stop their drawing to look.*)

Beth: You can feel something like a—it's not really a tail—bumps, like maybe a backbone.

Teacher: It's an interesting question. Most furry animals I've seen *do* have a tail. (*I notice that Lisa is erasing again, and beginning to look frustrated.*)

Teacher: Do you want another paper?

Lisa: No.

Teacher: The feet are definitely tricky to draw. From where I'm sitting I can only see one, and it looks like it's just toes sticking out of the body. I can't see the leg at all. Sometimes the way it looks seems strange in a drawing, or it's just hard to show. (*Lisa continues with her drawing, changes the angle of the foot she's working on, and seems more satisfied.*)

Later.

Teacher: Is it okay to add information that you know from reading a book to your observation? (*There are some nods of agreement, a few uh-huhs.*)

Teacher: How do scientists talk about that kind of information, so that people know that this information is something the scientist read, but not necessarily saw?

Susan: I read in a book.

Teacher: You know, Debbie, when they're writing those "distinguished" papers to share with other scientists, they name the book and even the page number they read the information on, so if any other scientist wants to go read it, she can.

Lisa: He's *still* drinking!

Teacher: He just keeps going and going.

Susan: Beth, that's good! I'm copying yours!

Teacher: What about Beth's drawing makes it look so realistic to you, Susan?

Susan: The shape!

Teacher: She's really found a way to show the shape. (*Several girls stop to take a look at Beth's drawing, then return to their own work.*)

This working period lasted a total of about twenty-five minutes. The work continued to be characterized by informal discussion about the guinea pig's behavior, each other's drawings, and related information. At the end of the period, most of the girls were ready to hand in their worksheets; several asked to continue their work later (Figure 4–2).

For this age group, as with the younger children, my availability was important. In interactions with children, I try to serve as a model, demonstrating ways of observing, recognizing and responding to children's observations, and resolving difficulties as they arise. Careful questions prompt children to clarify, analyze, extend, or reconsider aspects of their work. Through these discussions, they learn a way of working that is both scientific and enjoyable.

Figure 4–2	Guinea pig by Beth, age ten

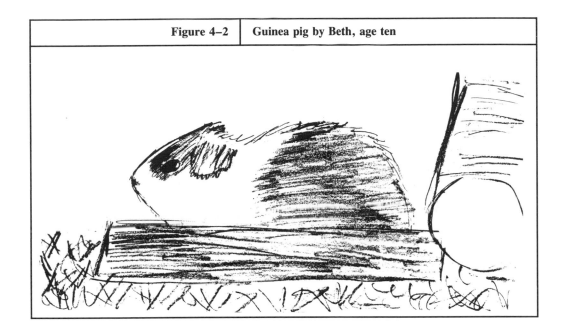

Another Science Meeting: Sharing Work

By the end of our first week of science, each child in the five- and six-year-old room had been to a beginning meeting, observed the guinea pig, and recorded some observations. Now it was time for us to meet together again and share work. I collected the observation sheets from the bulletin board and from the "Finished Work" pocket in the science area. Then I rang a bell—a signal for the children to stop and listen.

Teacher: Time to come to the rug for our Science Meeting. (*The children leave the different areas of the room where they have been working and begin to find places to sit on our meeting rug.*) "That's right, Lauric, we need to make this circle bigger. It needs to be big enough so everyone can fit, and everyone can see everyone else. (*There are some final adjustments—I wait until I see I have everyone's attention.*) Now you look ready to start!

After scientists have been working on a project for a while, they might go to a meeting. Sometimes scientists work on their own or with a team and sometimes they get together with lots of other scientists at a meeting. Sometimes the meeting has a special name, like "seminar" or "symposium" or "conference." We'll call ours a "Science Meeting." Why might scientists get together at a meeting?

Sara: They might want to share their work.

Teacher: Yes. That's an important reason to meet. Can you think of any others?

Timmy: To find out more stuff.

Teacher: Yes, they could find out more from other scientists. Our Science Meetings will be for the same things: for sharing work, and hearing about other people's work, and figuring things out together. Everyone observed the guinea pig this week. I saw you looking carefully at him and noticing how he moves and how he looks. Today, two people will get to share their observations. Then we'll list some things we know about our guinea pig. When it's someone's turn to share, that person will bring his or her work and come stand next to me. Amy, can you show us how to do that? (*Amy gets up, crosses circle, and stands next to me.*)

Teacher: An important job of the scientist sharing is to show her picture so that everyone in the circle can see it. Other scientists can learn by studying each other's drawings. Amy, can you find a way to stand right here, but show your picture to everyone? (*Amy shows her picture around.*)

Tracy: I didn't see.

Teacher: We do want everyone to be able to see! But it's easy when you're showing your work to miss someone. If you don't get a good look, what can you do?

Tracy: Ask her to see it.

Teacher: Yes. Show how you can get Amy's attention. (*Tracy raises her hand.*) Yes, it's so important to raise your hand! Amy could be feeling nervous up here, showing her work. And she has an important job to be concentrating on. What could happen if everyone just shouts out, "I can't see"?

Rachel: She might feel bad.

Danny: She could get mixed up.

Teacher: Right. So a way we can take care of Amy while she's sharing her work is to watch her show her picture, then raise our hands if we need a better look at it. Amy has another job at this meeting. She can say something she noticed about the guinea pig, or she can read what she wrote. Amy, which would you like to do?

Amy: Say it.

Teacher: Fine. Find a really big voice to say it with so everyone can hear.

Amy: I noticed he has toenails.

Teacher: Amy has shown us what the job of the scientist sharing is. Who knows what the job of the other scientists at the meeting is?

Randy: To listen.

Teacher: Yes. The other scientists will listen, so they can learn more about the guinea pig. And how will Amy know you are listening? (*Some kids shuffle, sit up straight, look at Amy.*)

Teacher: I see John doing something. John, what are you doing that shows Amy you're listening?

John: Not talking.

Teacher: I noticed that. What were you doing instead?

John: Looking at her.

Teacher: Yes. Looking at Amy. And holding your body . . .

John: Still!

Teacher: So the other scientists at the meeting are sitting still, and looking at Amy's picture, and listening when she talks. They also have another important job. They will be thinking about her work—thinking whether they understand it, whether they have a question or comment for her. Scientists want other people to understand their work. The comments we make show Amy what we understand. When you see Amy's picture, what's a comment you might have?

Kathleen: I like it.

Teacher: You think Amy did a good job drawing the guinea pig? (*Kathleen nods.*) How do you know if a science drawing is a good one?

Kathleen: If it looks like the real one.

Teacher: So scientists try to make their illustrations realistic. What did Amy show in her guinea pig that the real guinea pig has?

Kathleen: Fur!

Teacher: What color did she make the fur?

Sara: Brown and white.

Teacher: So a comment for Amy could be ''I notice you showed the guinea pig's brown-and-white fur'' or ''You drew fur like on the real guinea pig.'' Who's ready to practice a comment?

Brian: I notice you made his eyes.

Margaret: I notice you put the water bottle in.

Nicky: I like your picture. You made his nose!

Teacher: Those are all helpful comments for Amy. You might also have a question for Amy about her work. Maybe you notice she told about the guinea pig's toes and you want to know how she found out how many he had. How could you ask that?

John: How did you find out how much toes he has?

Amy: I counted when Ellen was holding him.

Teacher: You can also ask a question if you don't understand something, or if you couldn't hear or see. Anybody want to try?

Robbie: I didn't hear. Can you read it again?

Teacher: Is questions or comments a time I can say "I don't like your drawing" or "You forgot to show the ears?"

Children: No.

Teacher: How come?

Lisa: That would hurt someone's feelings.

Teacher: What if you were looking at my picture, and I really did forget the ears?

Randy: Just—say nothing!

Teacher: That would be taking good care of my feelings. Could you still make a comment, even if I forgot the ears?

Neil: Yes.

Teacher: What could you say?

Neil: You could just say about the other parts.

Teacher: OK. I think we're set. Now Amy is going to share her work for real. Amy, what will you need to do?

Amy: Show it so everyone can see.

Teacher: And what do all the scientists at the meeting need to do? Show me. Right. Be still and look at Amy.

Amy (*showing her picture*): I noticed he has toenails.

Teacher: You can ask for questions and comments if you want, Amy.

Amy: Any questions or comments? (*Amy calls on Jennifer.*)

Jennifer: I like your picture.

Amy: Thanks.

Teacher: Jennifer, what's one thing you see in Amy's picture that's like the real guinea pig?

Jennifer: She put the shape [Figure 5–1].

Teacher: She got the shape. Any other questions or comments?

Amy: Alex?

Alex: I noticed you showed his toes. (*Amy nods.*)

Teacher: One more question or comment for Amy.

Amy: Laurie?

Laurie: I made his ears pink, too.

Teacher: Thanks, Amy. I'll hold on to your work, and you can find your place on the meeting rug again. Who else is ready to share?

(*A dozen hands shoot up.*)

Teacher: I can see that *lots* of you are ready! We will be having another Science Meeting on Monday, so if you don't get a

Figure 5–1	**Guinea pig by girl, age six**

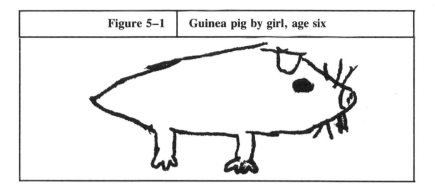

chance to share today, Monday will be another chance. Danny, it's your turn now.

(*Danny gets up to stand next to me. I hand him his observation sheet, and notice that a few quiet conversations have started up around the circle; Tracy is adjusting the velcro on her sneakers and Randy has shifted from sitting down to lying down.*)

Teacher (*to Danny*): I see you are ready to begin. You'll know everyone is ready to listen when you see that everyone is sitting still and looking at you. (*Danny looks around the circle of children. Randy sits up, Tracy sticks her velcro in place, and Danny holds out his picture for everyone to see.*)

Teacher: What's something you noticed when you looked at the guinea pig, Danny?

Danny: He squeaks.

Teacher: When you're ready, you can ask for questions or comments.

Danny: I'm ready for questions and comments. Joel?

Joel: What's that part in the middle?

Danny: Here? (*Joel nods.*) That's his heart. It's on the inside. Kate?

Kate: I can't see. (*Danny turns his paper and points out the heart to Kate.*)

Danny: Laurie?

Laurie: I like your picture and he can squeak loud!

Danny: I know!

Teacher: One more question or comment for Danny.

Danny: Michael?

Michael: I notice you made his eyes.

Teacher: Thanks, Danny. I'll hang on to your paper. (*Danny finds* *his place, and I move the chart stand closer to the meeting so everyone can see it.*)

Teacher: I'm going to use this paper to keep track of some of the observations you have made. You told me that scientists discover things, and this week you have made many discoveries about the guinea pig. I'll start with Amy's observation. (*I write and then read.*) The guinea pig has toenails. (*I continue, adding Danny's observation.*) He squeaks. Who else noticed something I can add to the list? Rachel?

Rachel: He has three toes on the back but not on the front.

Teacher: Do you remember how many are on the front?

Rachel: I think four.

John: That's right, four.

Teacher: Did anybody else notice that?

Children: I did! I knew that! (*I hear many replies.*)

Teacher: Sara, what did you notice?

Sara: His ears flop in a little at the top.

(I continue to call on children, and add their observations to the list. In a few minutes, the chart paper is nearly full. Some children still have hands raised, ready with yet another discovery, but yawns and wiggles tell me it's time to move on.)

Teacher: This is a long list! You have figured out lots of important things about our guinea pig by observing him this week. I will save this list, and we can add more to it at our next meeting. And we can put this work you've finished up on the science bulletin board. You can look at it to find out even more about the guinea pig! At this meeting, I saw how carefully you can listen when another scientist is sharing work. That is another important way scientists can learn.

With older children, the format of the first Science Meeting is basically the same as for fives and sixes. Children can collect their own work from the finished work box or display and gather in a circle. Some children will have the chance to share their observation sheets, others to contribute questions and comments. I may choose to list one observation from each child at this meeting, or I may do that at a later time. Children familiar with the writing process will find that the feel of this meeting is also familiar, and they will bring to their science work the ability to listen to and learn from each other that they've developed through their work as writers. (See the Bibliography for books about the writing process.) The basic pattern of sharing followed by questions and comments is the same at all ages, as in this example of Marion, age eight, sharing at a Science Meeting:

Marion: I looked at a feather. (*Reading from her worksheet*) ''The bottom has white fluffy things. The shaft looks like plastic. One side is darker than the other side. The shaft gets smaller when it goes up. The feather looks like a paddle. On one side it has a white outline but on the other side it doesn't have the outline.'' Questions or comments?

Andrea: I like your picture. It's realistic.

Chip: You showed all of the different colors.

Teacher: Can you tell people again, Marion, that word for this plasticky part?

Marion: The shaft.

Teacher: The shaft.

Jay: I saw that feather and I think your picture really looks like it [Figure 5–2].

Figure 5–2	Feather painting by Marion, age eight

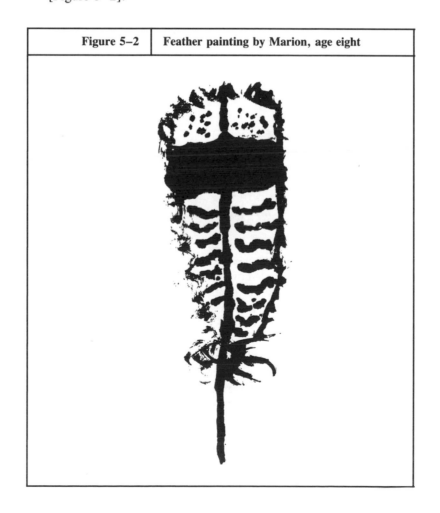

The Teacher's Role During Science Meetings

In the preceding examples children met to share their worksheets and to exchange information about their observations. Children can also meet to solve problems, plan trips, or define research questions. Whatever the case, skillful management by the teacher helps ensure meetings that are productive and positive.

As teacher, I determined when we would start our science work but the children helped to define what that work would be, and what procedures or rules would help us carry out the work in our room. Similar collaboration is critical in this first sharing meeting. The group needs to have a sense of purpose; they need to understand how this meeting relates to their science work. A group of young or inexperienced children may not have much of a sense about why scientists would come together in a meeting. In that case it's fine for the teacher to explain (clearly and briefly) the point: "This is our meeting for sharing science work. When scientists meet like this, they can find out about new discoveries and discuss their ideas." Children can add to the teacher's definition or restate it: "They go to the meeting so they can learn more."; "They go to tell what they noticed."

Older children (who may have some sense that adult researchers meet and discuss work—or who may have worked in this cooperative, collaborative fashion in another subject area) are usually ready with reasons why scientists might choose to meet. They realize that scientists need to come together to get help from one another, share discoveries, and solve problems.

I want the tone of this meeting to be one of interest and excitement. The best meetings are lively ones, with everyone participating. Part of what I'm doing at the meeting is expressing my own curiosity, excitement, and eagerness. It's not an act. I'm just making clear my attitudes about science generally, and about the specific work our class is doing. I'm also setting up a situation (both at the science table and at this meeting) that supports the notion that science involves interesting events, thought-provoking problems, and phenomena children can understand.

Another important part of tone that is related to interest and excitement is safety. The meeting needs to be a place where any child can bring work and receive the respectful attention of classmates as well as the teacher, free from ridicule and judgment. Different ways of thinking and different kinds of products must be accepted.

Knowing that kind of safety is available enables children to take the risk of exposing their thinking, showing their work, or struggling with ideas that may be unclear or evolving. I want the meeting to be a dynamic place where children can grapple with ideas about the things they've observed, so working to establish a tone of excitement and safety is my first priority.

Some of the many specifics that contribute to a positive meeting tone and encourage interested attentiveness, collegial sharing, and discussion are described here.

The teacher is clear about the purpose of the meeting. My own clarity helps me keep the meeting focused and know what sort of discussion to encourage and what to stop. After I've worked with the children to define our purpose, they can take responsibility for the meeting as well.

Teacher and children define behavioral expectations together. Since statements of purpose tend to be general, I need to figure out what specific behaviors will help make our meeting productive. The children can help define these, and we will all need to practice. The more that rules arise as children's solutions to problems, or potential problems, the more we can expect children to understand and take responsibility for following rules. Rules that are imposed from outside, or that seem arbitrary, unconnected to a real issue, are difficult for children to remember and to follow. With help, children can define a set of rules or expectations that help them feel safe and productive at meeting.

Another thing that contributes to a positive tone is the way the teacher behaves. If the teacher is clearly excited about the material being discussed, open to learning from her own observations and from listening to and watching students, children will see this. Her attitude may free them to be excited and attentive. Body language is important in showing interest. If a child is sharing work at a meeting, an interested teacher looks at the child's work. She may need to glance around the meeting from time to time to see how children are doing with the meeting rules, but she devotes most of her attention to the work of that child. Maybe she leans in for a better look, or has a thoughtful question to ask about the work, or a comment about the parts that interest her. A very different statement is made if she turns her attention elsewhere—writing, talking to another child or teacher, counting lunch money, or dealing with a management issue.

An extension of this point is the need for consistency between the teacher's behavior and the behavior expected from the children. Our jobs are not entirely the same, of course. (The teacher, for example, may not sit for half an hour at the science table drawing the guinea pig.) However, we are in this classroom together, and this science work will only be exciting if we care about it together. If I say "Scientists are curious," but I am not showing curiosity, children will perceive this inconsistency. I need to show, as well as say, how that looks.

Teacher uses clear, positive language. I need to help the children state the purpose of the meeting and the rules of the meeting in language that is specific, clear, and *positive*. When I ask how we can take care of the feelings of a child sharing his observation, children tend to respond: ''Don't laugh at their picture''; ''Don't talk while they're having their turn.''

I need to help children restate these behaviors in terms of what we *will* do: ''That's right. We can't pay good attention if we're talking, so we look carefully at the picture and we listen.'' We come together to share, to think, to learn, to figure things out. I don't want to dwell on negative behaviors.

Teacher concentrates on only one or two behaviors or skills per meeting. In the early meetings, I concentrate my attention on one or two issues, such as what children do while someone is sharing. We begin by quickly reviewing those behaviors at the start of the meeting. Then during the course of the meeting, I'll note the positive work I see children doing: ''I notice you looking right at Annie, Jason. That tells her you are ready to hear about her discovery.'' I refrain from excessive comments about other issues (for example, the accuracy of the observations, the quality of questions and comments) until another time, when one of *those* is my main focus. When children are learning and practicing new ways of working together, focusing on one issue or behavior at a time keeps the work manageable. If I try to attend to everything at once, the children (and I) will soon be overwhelmed. I work at a slow pace, with one focus first, then another. This pace will allow all of us to develop our skills and recognize our accomplishments.

There are many possible children's skills and behaviors that could be the focus of a Science Meeting. You might try to have the children do the following:

Learn to read an observation with a big voice.

Practice thoughtful questions and comments.

Pool or list all the information that has been gathered.

Learn to handle a new pet.

Decide together what to do next.

Teacher reinforces positive behavior and contributions. During the meeting, I will comment on the positive behavior I see. Maintaining the tone I want takes deliberate, conscientious effort, especially during the first few meetings. If I set out expectations about behavior but then quickly shift all of my attention to content discussions, and let this inappropriate behavior or that helpful behavior go unnoticed, then the tone of the meeting will deteriorate rapidly. Soon I will be forced to shift my attention away from the guinea pig and onto the ''fooling around,'' because fooling will have become disruptive. Alternatively, I may observe no significant disruptive behavior, but wonder why the meeting feels so ''flat''—why only a few children are participating.

If I can balance my attention so that I can help children think and talk about their work with the guinea pig, but also continue to "take the pulse" of the meeting, noting with words or a look when a positive contribution is made, then an upbeat, excited, interested tone is possible.

Teacher chooses responses with care. The meeting is a forum where children will share their observations. This demands certain kinds of responses from the teacher and excludes others. I may choose to reflect what I've heard the child say, or what I've noticed in the drawing: "You saw that the guinea pig has little claws"; "You looked to see if the guinea pig has a tail." I avoid "correcting" work with comments like "You showed a pink guinea pig, but ours is brown" or "Guinea pigs do not have tails."

Many of us were schooled in situations where science experiments had to have a certain outcome to be "right," or where our job, dissecting the frog, was to find and label the organs the textbook assured us were there. There may be many points at which such work is useful, but it is not what we are doing prior to or at this meeting. As teachers, we need to take care that our responses are not "textbook" responses or corrective judgments. The more we were raised with "unsatisfactory," "A," "B," "C+," "beautiful drawing," "wrong answer," the easier it is to slip into that role as the person in charge of this meeting.

If we can keep ourselves focused on the real purpose of this work, we can encourage divergent thinking and open sharing of observations and ideas. If the meeting becomes a place to go to have work evaluated, we'll lose the independent thinking we want to see children developing.

Teacher helps children see what they have learned. The teacher can help children articulate or demonstrate their discoveries. She can also help keep track of observations, ideas, or questions. There are many ways to do this. Listing children's observations on a chart for everyone to see creates a record of discoveries and shows by its very length how much children know. Repeating something a child has shared can underline a discovery for that child as well as for the group. "You noticed the guinea pig has no tail" and "Can you tell people again that word for the plasticky part of your feather?" are examples of this. Teachers can ask questions to draw out ideas or questions that may have come up during a work time; they can also help children organize information so that it is easier to make sense of and use it. In science it is important to articulate what you have seen, what connections you are making, what questions you have. Teachers can help children do this.

Teachers manage transitions. The meeting needs to have a defined beginning and end, labeled by the teacher. If the lunch bell rings and children scramble to get on line, the feelings of the child in the midst of sharing work will be hurt. Meetings that "trickle off" (as a few children get fidgety) or are crowded up against a deadline (such as the dismissal bell) deteriorate towards the end. I try to label the start of the meeting and to let the children know (maybe even practice) how to get needed materials and assemble on time. Similarly, I need to let them know how the meeting will end, and how the transition out of the meeting will occur.

Teachers match meeting length with children's capabilities. Teachers need to be aware of the length of time a particular age group and class can be expected to focus at a meeting. It's not an easy thing to come to a meeting, sit still in a group with a lot of other people, and devote your attention to someone else's work, ideas or questions. It's taxing. I think we can expect children to do it and to do a good job of it, but for limited periods of time. Many young children can manage a fifteen-minute meeting; for others, ten minutes is enough. While some children may be able to stay involved for much longer periods of time (I have seen a group of seven-year-olds excited and involved for forty minutes), I need to monitor the meeting carefully so that the tone stays positive. Once children have exceeded their limits, it will be very difficult to keep the meeting interesting and productive.

Teachers give high priority to classroom management. It may seem as though an enormous amount of time at the beginning of the year is devoted to issues of management, rather than discussion, experimentation, and all kinds of juicy science content. (Someone draws a guinea pig with a long furry tail, and I attend instead to whether or not that child raises her hand before making a comment at meeting.) In fact, it may seem as though I am spending forever discussing management in a book that is supposed to be about teaching science. But to separate completely the content of science from the management of the classroom would be an oversimplification of teaching.

We are teaching children. We explore science with them. And so for me, science content and the context in which we work to understand it are not separable. Worthwhile subject matter must be a part of our science program from the beginning. Otherwise, we cannot expect children to invest in working, thinking, or attending at meetings. Eleanor Duckworth, in her review of the African Primary Science Program, writes: "I react strongly against the thought that we need to provide children with only a set of intellectual processes—a dry, contentless set of tools that they can go about applying. I believe that the tools cannot help developing once children have something real to think about; and if they don't have anything real to think about, they won't be applying tools anyway" (1978, 27).

I agree. I also believe that what we teach and how we teach (or what we learn and how we learn) are connected. Just as children must have worthwhile content to think about in order to invest their energy in learning, they must have a classroom environment in which thinking and working are possible. Children unused to cooperating, collaborating, and considering each others' ideas will need to learn new ways of working together as they go about the business of observing and discovering the phenomena of the world around them. Careful attention at the beginning of the year to "how to be together at meeting" helps insure a dependable and respectful working climate, and leaves teacher and children increasingly able to focus on interesting scientific observations and questions as the year progresses.

Meetings follow a predictable format. The more the meeting follows a predictable pattern, the more children can be free to think, discuss, and attend. The format of the meetings I've described may at first seem unnecessarily formal or ritualized. However, I believe that all this structure provides both teacher and children with great freedom. After two or three meetings, five-year-olds know what to expect. They can count on safety when they share, a chance to listen to and comment on others' work, and they know this meeting will end before recess, in time to go out and play. Energy that might be spent guessing or worrying about expectations or what will happen next now is available for thinking about what we've discovered about the guinea pig. Children at seven and eight can not only participate in such a meeting, they can run it. Lucy Calkins writes:

> I have finally realized that the most creative environments in our society are not the kaleidoscopic environments in which everything is always changing and complex. They are, instead, the predictable and consistent ones: the scholar's library, the researcher's laboratory, the artist's studio. Each of these environments is deliberately kept *predictable* and *simple* because the work at hand and the changing interactions around the work are so unpredictable and complex. (1986, 12)

Some Additional Guidelines for Science Meetings

Sharing drawing, writing, or ideas is a child's choice. Although many children will be dying to share, some will be anxious and hang back. Give these children some time. There may be different reasons for hanging back. Learning disabled children or any children who are not happy with the way their drawing or writing looks may be reluctant to share. These children may need help to see the value of their products and permission to limit their sharing to part of their work for a time.

Beginning readers or writers (whether because of age or a disability) can choose to read or say something they discovered, or to have a teacher help with the reading.

Some children need to watch for a while before they try anything. Once they have decided the situation is safe or have learned how to share from observing others, they'll be ready for a turn.

Respectful meeting behavior should be expected of *all* children, but a particular level of participation may be easier for one child than another. Some children rush to volunteer; others need to be asked specifically, "You haven't had the chance to share your observation yet, Lisa. Do you want a turn today?"

If weeks go by and a child still is unwilling to share, and it seems that the meeting truly is a place where children's feelings will be protected if they risk sharing, then it's time to talk further with that child, his or her parents, or other teachers to find out more about what is going on.

Finally, when we can recognize and appreciate each child's unique contribution to this work, and we communicate our observations clearly, without comparing one child to another, we contribute to a spirit of cooperative research, and respect for different ways of working and thinking. I am surprised at the number of science programs at the elementary school level that have been developed for a narrowly defined population of "gifted and talented" students. In reflecting on the science work of the particular five- and six-year-old group I've described here, I see that the guinea pig is often jumpy and even bites, but that whenever Rachel picks him up, he settles down quietly in her arms. I also notice that Brian has drawn a picture that astonishes us all. We are amazed at the likeness between his drawing and the real guinea pig. Then there is Eileen, who seems so often to get us started on making a connection, or figuring out how to answer a question. Her ideas usually lack a certain practicality ("Well, if we want to know what wild guinea pigs eat, we should go to the country where they really live and just find some and see what they like to eat!"), but once her imaginative chatter gets us thinking, another child is quick to formulate an adaptation of her idea that we can actually try. I see many different gifts and talents, each important to our progress in this science work.

6

Extending Science Work: Teacher As Facilitator

When we give up teaching from textbooks, we give up the comfort of knowing stock answers for stock questions. We give our attention to children as they work, supporting their efforts and enabling them to move ahead with their ideas and projects. Children, free to pursue their own questions, head off in various directions. The situations that result may be expected and familiar or they may take us by surprise. Knowing how to look at children's work and figuring out what sort of response will be helpful in each unique situation becomes our challenge.

The art of understanding what children are trying to express and responding appropriately is not a simple business, but it is not an entirely mysterious one either. Many teachers have found ways to help children get interested, develop objectivity or persistence, articulate questions, take pride in their work, or overcome fears. These teachers may operate intuitively, following hunches or feelings, or they may work consciously and deliberately with theory in mind, analyzing situations and planning out their responses. In either case, we can learn much about what helps children from observing our own—and others'—interactions in the classroom. We can draw on this understanding when we next find ourselves in the midst of a science meeting or when we watch a child observe at the science table.

This chapter contains many examples of classroom work, which I hope will illuminate some of the principles that can guide us as we interact with children during their science studies. Your own experiments will lead you to even more.

Helping Children to Answer Their Own Questions

Children raise many questions that they can answer for themselves through their own observations and experiences. When we help children draw on their own resources to solve problems, we help them learn, for it is their own activity that teaches them most effectively. We also help them to develop the independence and competence that will enable them to act rather than feel overwhelmed or frustrated when confronted with questions.

Opportunities to turn children's questions over to them to answer frequently arise. In the following example, five-year-old Joshua was looking rather uneasily at the guinea pig, considering, I suspect, whether or not to pat it.

Josh: Does he have teeth?

Teacher: You can check and see. I'll hold him up so you can see his mouth better.

Josh: He does! Long teeth!

Teacher: He uses those teeth to eat. But if you're worried that he might bite you instead of his food, I'll hold him like this—facing me—and you can touch him here on his back.

On another occasion, Janet, age seven, was wondering about her cricket.

Janet: How do they chirp?

Teacher: Let's watch your cricket for a few minutes. Maybe we'll be able to tell.
(*We watch. Eventually the cricket chirps again.*)

Janet: I saw it! When it chirped, it kind of chattered its wings!

In both of these examples children raised questions to which their own observations provided the answers. Not all questions in science can be explored by simply taking another look, but those that can be should be given over to children to answer. Note that in the above examples I did not tease the children, making a game of withholding information that they had requested. I encouraged them to see for themselves and I supported them as they tried.

Another opportunity to encourage children to find their own answers occurred one morning when a class of eight-year-olds arrived at school to discover a hole chipped in one of the chicken eggs they were incubating. They could see a chick's beak pushing at the shell. Although they watched for half an hour, the chick succeeded in widening its hole only slightly (Figure 6–1).

Figure 6–1	Drawing by boy, age eight

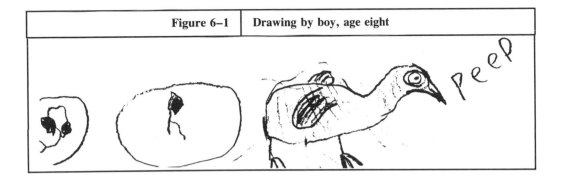

Erin: How long does it take them to hatch?

Teacher: This chick doesn't seem to be getting out very fast, does it? Is there a way you could find out how long it takes?

Erin: Well, we could just keep on watching it. We could write down what the time was when we noticed it was hatching and the time when it's hatched.

Carla: Then we could figure out how much time had gone by.

Teacher: And if you need to take a break from watching to go do something else for a while?

Adam: We could keep coming back to check. Like at the end of each period, or every ten minutes or something.

Teacher: That sounds like a plan that will work.

Days later the children got out a book about chickens and read:

> After three weeks' incubation, the chick is ready to emerge. It jabs at the underside of the shell with a special egg tooth on its beak, working its way around the middle of the egg. This process is known as "pipping" and can take anywhere from twenty minutes to fourteen hours to complete. (Oxford Scientific Films 1979, 3)

This information was an exciting find, as it both confirmed and extended the children's own firsthand research. I think that this information would have been received quite differently had it been given to the children before their own direct experience with chicks hatching and before they themselves had raised the question "How long does it take?" It would have been less exciting and less meaningful if it had been disconnected from a real event.

Teachers can encourage children both to use their senses to gather information and then to use the information they have gathered.

One fall I took a class hiking along a shallow stream. The children spread out to explore. Some discovered tiny creatures in the shallow water, others pointed out special rocks or brightly colored mushrooms. Holly bent down to inspect something. I joined a group of children assembling around her where she knelt beside the brown, dry, spore-bearing stalk of a sensitive fern (Figure 6–2).

Holly: What's *that* thing?

Darcy: I think it's dead.

BK: Is it a plant?

Jess: I think I've seen one of those before, but I don't know what they are.

Teacher: Let's see what you've found.

Holly: This thing.

Teacher: That's interesting. Do you want to bring it back to school so you can look at it more and try to find out what it is?

Holly: Well, yes, but what if it's rare? I know some flowers are rare and you're not supposed to pick them.

Teacher: That's a good point. We shouldn't pick it if it's rare. Is there a way you can find out if it's rare here?

Holly: Well, we could look around and see if there are any more.

Teacher: Okay. Let me know what you find. (*The children fan out and search. They find several groups of the strange brown things—dozens of stalks in all.*)

Teacher: So you found quite a few?

BK: Thirty, maybe more.

Darcy: (*laughing*): I don't think they're too rare, at least not here!

Teacher: What does that make you think, Holly?

Figure 6–2	Drawing of a sensitive fern stalk by girl, age eight

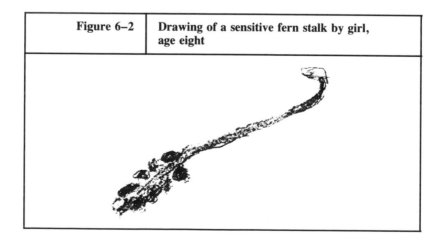

Holly: That I could pick one or two to bring back.

Teacher: But if you hadn't found very many?

Holly: Then it might be rare and we shouldn't pick any.

My idea, here, was to help the children see what they knew (the meaning of rarity, the ethics of picking rare flowers or plants) and use their understanding to solve Holly's problem: she wanted to pick a stalk but didn't know if she should.

The matter could have been settled more quickly by my saying "I don't think this is rare. Go ahead and pick it." One advantage of not making this decision for Holly and instead allowing the group to figure out how to determine whether the stalk was "too rare" to pick was that another time they might be able to use this experience to deal with a similar problem. If the solution depended on my particular knowledge or permission, it would not be transferable. (Of course, there are times when it may be important to establish collection rules and then share your thinking with the children. For instance, in a sanctuary, you may be responsible for enforcing a "no picking" rule or you may need to dissuade a determined child from bringing home a baby bird.)

Further Research

Sometimes experiments can be devised to help children find out about the things that puzzle them. This was my solution for a small group of eight-year-olds who were forcing tulip bulbs. They had carefully observed and drawn the bulbs they had selected, and then planted them in clay pots filled with potting soil. The pots were put in an unheated part of the school building for two cold weeks in February, then brought into the classroom and watered.

After just a few days of warmth and water the children noticed tiny green sprouts in the pots. "Our tulips are growing!" they announced with excitement. Over the next few days, more green sprouts appeared, more by far than the number of bulbs that had been planted. The children watched as tiny paired leaves developed on each sprout (Figure 6–3).

"These don't look that much like tulips," Ginger said skeptically.

"They look like weeds!" remarked Nathan.

"You're right! They do look like weeds," Charlene nodded.

The children came to report their new idea to me.

"So you think these things that are growing in your pots aren't

| Figure 6–3 | The Tulip Journal by Ginger, age eight |

A: Tulip bulbs before being planted

1.

2.

B: Weeds start growing

There's some kind of groth!

I Think it might be a weed but maybe not!

C: Third petal starts growing

It still has That Groth But it's growing a 3rd pedale

Finaly my tulip's growing! Yea!

Helping Children to Answer Their Own Questions

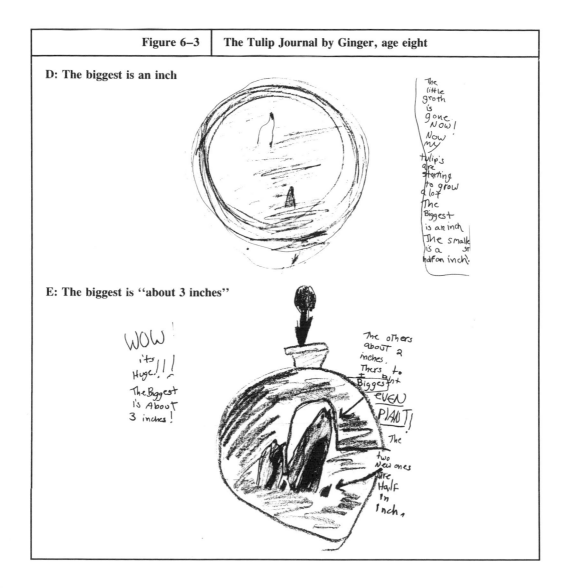

| Figure 6–3 | The Tulip Journal by Ginger, age eight |

D: The biggest is an inch

The little groth is gone Now! Now my tulip's are starting to grow a lot The Biggest is an inch The small is a st hdf on inch!

E: The biggest is "about 3 inches"

WOW! it's Huge!!! The Biggest Is About 3 inches!

The others about 2 inches. Thers to bight Biggest EVEN PLANT! The two New ones are Half 'n Inch.

tulips after all, but are something else?"

"Yes, aren't they?"

"Well, what have you observed that makes you think so?"

"They look just like weeds," Nathan explained.

"And besides, there's too many of them. I have four growing in my pot but I only planted two tulip bulbs," continued Patrick.

"And they aren't growing in the right places, either," Charlene added.

I considered this information. "I can see why you think they might be weeds instead of tulips," I said. "Can you think of a way to find out for sure?"

A few ideas were proposed: digging up the tiny sprouts to see whether they were growing out of the tulip bulbs, comparing the sprouts to some other weeds, and so on. In the end, the children decided that the simplest solution would be to continue with the daily observations and see if anything else grew in the pots.

Nearly two weeks after the first green sprouts appeared, the children discovered new, larger sprouts pushing out of the soil. These looked more like tulips, they all agreed.

Discussing observations once more, I came back to a question that had been brought up earlier by one of the children but then forgotten. "How did those weeds end up growing in your flower pots? Did you plant them?"

Of course, they had not; they had planted only tulip bulbs. But they did have some ideas about how such a thing could have happened.

"Maybe some weed seeds were in the dirt to begin with. Then when we watered the dirt they just started growing," Nathan suggested.

"Or maybe some seeds blew in from somewhere else," Ginger proposed.

I might have chosen to voice my support for these explanations and then let the whole thing go, but instead I pushed for confirmation. "How could you find out if your hypotheses are correct?" I asked. "Both ideas sound like possible explanations for what happened. Is there a way to be more sure?"

"You'd have to do an experiment," Ginger stated.

"What sort of experiment might work?" I asked.

There were no responses.

"Well, let's look at this first hypothesis," I went on. "Nathan thought that maybe there were some weed seeds in the dirt to begin with. How could you tell if there were?"

"You could look at the dirt," Ricky suggested. "You could put some under the microscope and see if you see any seeds."

"That sounds like a big job," I said, "but worth a try."

"Or we could just look around in the dirt," Nathan offered. "Maybe we would find some seeds."

"We could borrow a sifter from another class," said Patrick, "They have sifters in the sand table. Remember? We used to use them."

"You have a few ideas to work on to try to see if the hypothesis about weeds seeds being in the potting soil might be true. Is there anything else you want to try?"

"I have an idea!" said Charlene. "We could fill a pot up with dirt, but not plant anything in the dirt. Then we could water it and see if anything grows."

Reports of the children's work follow.

We had a hypothesis that there was a seed in the soil that we were using for our tulips. Me and Patrick got a sifter and started sifting through the dirt. Lo and behold we found a little weed that was attached to a seed. Our hypothesis was right. (Ricky, age eight)

We planted soil to see if anything was in the soil because little green plants were growing in our tulip pots that we didn't plant, we wanted to know what they were. The results were: nothing grew. The reason we think is there wasn't any seed in the part of the soil we planted but there were in other parts. (Ginger, age eight, and Charlene, age seven)

I have warned against withholding answers to children's questions in a teasing manner. Pretending not to know something that one in fact knows is apt to be confusing to children. We need not worry about having enough opportunity to encourage children to find their own answers. However great our knowledge, children walking in the woods or observing at the science table are sure to uncover something that is mysterious to us, too. Quite often, children are so absorbed with their own questions and puzzles that they do not even look to us for answers. I did not need to worry about whether or not to tell Holly the name of her brown stalk was "sensitive fern," for her wondering "What is it?" was more an exclamation of discovery than a request for a label. She did not follow up by coming to me and directly asking for it to be named. Even if she had, the mystery would hardly have been solved, for this dry brown thing looked nothing like a fern—it didn't even seem alive.

When we hand children's questions back to them to answer and they intently go off to "have another look," or breathlessly return to share their latest findings, then we have been helpful. If they seem confused, frustrated, or impatient with us, then perhaps the situation calls for another response. Teacher Carolyn Pratt writes:

The over-helpful adult is no help, is actually a hindrance to the child. What perceptive adult has not seen a child's face go blank like a closed door at the very moment when he is receiving the most helpful attention? Who has not had the humiliating experience of having a child walk idly away in the middle of an answer to his question?

She continues:

Questions came in a steady stream from some of my children when we first began to go on our trips. But when they got their questions turned back to them—"Why do *you* think the ferry has two round ends?"—they were silenced for a while. When the questions came again they were different. They were not asked just to get attention, to make conversation, or for the dozen reasons besides that of gaining information. They were sincere and purposeful; the question now became what it should be, the first step in the child's own effort to find the answer for himself. . . .

The answer which the child has found out for himself is the one which has meaning for him, both in the information gained and in the experience of finding it. (Pratt 1948, 44–45)

Providing Direct Instruction or Information

Though I often turn children's questions back over to them, there are times when a direct answer is more helpful.

I was working on an art project with a group of five-year-olds when Angie, a seven-year-old student from another class, hurried into the room. She stood at my side, shifting from foot to foot as I finished helping Jordan with his print making.

"Yes, Angie?" I looked up.

"Well," she began with intensity, "you know how our class is studying pond animals? We brought back a frog, and I've been noticing it has these two big circles on his head. Do you know what they are?"

"Big circles, two of them?" I repeated. Angie nodded vigorously.

"I think I can help. Did you make a picture of how they look?"

Again she nodded. "Do you want me to get it?"

"I'd love that!" I replied. "That would really help me be sure." She returned in a moment, breathless. I studied her drawing (Figure 6–4).

"Here?" I pointed, "right behind its eyes?"

She nodded yes. "Do you know what they are?"

"Well, this may seem strange, but those circles are your frog's ears."

Angie looked at her picture, then at me, incredulous.

"They aren't much like your ears, are they?" I asked.

Angie laughed, "No!"

"Well," I explained, "your ears have this big part on the outside that we can see, and other parts, like the eardrum, inside. But frogs don't have the big outside part. They hear with those two circles you discovered."

Angie returned to her room where, her teacher reported, she spent most of the afternoon looking at books about frogs, studying the pictures and copying them onto drawing paper.

Direct answers, such as the one I gave Angie, are often required. In some cases, it is better to hand the question back to the child, but in this case I chose to give a direct answer for several reasons. It was evident to me that Angie had already taken her observation work quite far. She'd gone beyond recognizing all the familiar frog things—eyes, legs, greenness, and so forth and she had identified a part that was mysterious to her. She wanted to know what those big circles were! Her interest in finding out about them was strong enough to cause her to seek me (a teacher in another classroom). Had there been a way to provide Angie with an experience that might have led her to discover for herself what those two circles were, I'd have wanted to provide it. However, I could think of no way for her direct investigation to yield the information she sought. She now either had to search through books for the answer or ask someone. Either would have been a valid choice.

Figure 6–4	Drawing of a frog by Angie (seven years): note ears!

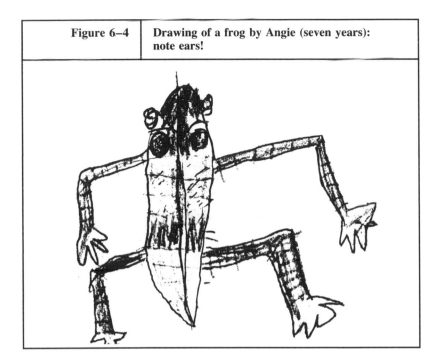

Angie's age, reading ability, urgency, and the fact that I knew a little about frog ears steered me toward a direct answer.[1]

It is worth noting Angie's reaction to hearing that she had discovered frog's ears. Rather than feeling "done" or losing interest, she spent the rest of the day in self-designed frog research.

Respecting Children's Questions

If a question is important to a child, then it is a good question to pursue. As teachers, we have to keep this in mind, for the questions children raise are not always the ones we would raise for them.

About a week after Angie discovered frog ears, she was back in my classroom again. "Do you know about frog's tongues?" she in-

---

[1]I felt sure that the circles Angie had discovered were frog ears. But more often than not I am unsure of the answers to children's questions. It is surely unhelpful to give misinformation as though it were correct. It is helpful, however, for children to hear us acknowledge, comfortably and directly, when we don't know something, and to join with them in a search for the answer.

quired. It wasn't a question I'd been expecting. I was tempted to joke. Luckily I didn't.

"Frog's tongues?" I echoed.

"I want to know about frog's tongues," she asserted. "What they're really like. Can you help me?"

I arranged to meet her later in the day when I had a break (so important was this question that she was willing to give up recess to meet me). Angie's class had set up a large aquarium as temporary home for two frogs, soon to be returned to the pond where they'd been collected. Angie and I wet our hands, and drew one out. Angie helped me hold the frog securely while I pushed up on its upper "lip." Eventually it gulped and opened its mouth, revealing its throat and tongue. Angie saw the tongue was attached at the front, pinkish, and, to her surprise, thick and fat looking.

"Can we show everyone else?" she pleaded.

"I'll put the frog back for now, and we can try to figure out a way that can work." We did manage to give everyone a quick peek as they filed in from recess. A few, like Angie, were particularly intrigued. Angie's original curiosity had been aroused by seeing pictures of frogs in books, frogs snapping flies out of the air with their long, sticky tongues. She couldn't figure out how all that tongue could fit back inside a frog's mouth. Seeing the real frog's tongue was even more puzzling. How could that short, fat tongue reach out and catch a fly? A group of children worked with the idea for a while, considering the way they could change the shape of their own tongues, and thinking how it might work to attach them in front.

When Angie first brought me her question, I had no idea where this work would lead. In fact, it wasn't until after we had looked together at the frog's tongue and I was listening to children discussing their reactions and ideas that I began to understand the thinking that had prompted her question in the first place and began to see how this experience might be put to use. I've yet to come across a textbook or curriculum guide that recommends a look at frog tongues as part of a second-grade science program, and I know it might seem like a pointless or silly activity for school. But Angie wanted to know about them. She thought of the question herself, and she deserved to have her work taken seriously.

Beginning Research

A class of seven- and eight-year-old children who had been observing crickets on a daily basis—describing them, drawing them, and noting behaviors—met one afternoon to share findings. I listed each discovery on our chart as it was reported.

Ben: I noticed that my cricket has little hairs on its legs.

Kim: Mine does, too. I think they all have that.

Bonnie: They have designs on the wings.

Karin: Some of the crickets chirp, but not all of them.

Marty: They have long feelers that look as if they come out of their eyes.

Beth: I noticed that my cricket has two eyes.

Jeff: Some have two little tails on the back, and some have the two little tails with one big tail in the middle.

Jackie: My cricket has four eyes.

Teacher: Wait a minute. When Beth looked at her cricket, she found two eyes. When Jackie looked, she found four! Did anyone else see eyes on a cricket?

Nicky: Mine had two.

Maureen: Mine, too!

Lynnie: I think mine has four.

Jeff: Mine definitely had two.

Greg: I think that they have lots and lots of eyes—they have a special kind of eyes.

Teacher: Compound eyes?

Greg: That's it.

Teacher: Claudia, you look puzzled.

Claudia: But how do you know where the eyes are? I didn't see *any* eyes!

Douglas: They're on the head—one on each side—right where the feelers are.

Claudia: But how can you tell those are eyes? Just because our eyes are on our heads doesn't mean a cricket's are!

Teacher: You have noticed many things about our crickets during the past several days. And it seems there are some questions about the eyes. Some of you counted two, and some of you counted four. Greg thinks there might be lots and lots—that crickets might have a special kind of eyes called "compound eyes." Claudia is wondering how we can be sure the things we are seeing really are the eyes. How will we find out?

Kim: We could look more closely.

Teacher: A closer look might help. And how could you look more closely?

Marty: Well, we could try the microscope or maybe a magnifying glass.

Teacher: Good ideas. We can try to take a closer look tomorrow. But how will we figure out if the things we think are the eyes really *are* the eyes?

Casey: We could look it up in a book.

Teacher: What kind of a book do you think would help us?

Casey: Well, that book Keith brought in. It tells about insects. Or maybe one of the other books on the science table.

Teacher: Okay, that's another good idea for tomorrow. You can look and see if any of our books tell about cricket eyes. So far, you've told me that one way to find out more about cricket eyes is to observe the crickets again and to look more closely. Another way is to look in books. Are there any other ways that we could research or try to find out?

Richie: We could just ask someone who knows!

Teacher: Another good idea. Scientists often talk to other people to get information. Who might know about crickets?

Karin: You might!

Teacher: Yes, I *am* interested in crickets! And I've been observing them just like you have, so I know some things. But I'm not sure about the eyes. At first I thought there were two, but then lots of you have been showing me some little spots that might be more eyes. And like Greg, I've heard about those special compound eyes, but Claudia's question has me wondering, too! So we'll have to find someone else who can help. Who else could we try?

Sean: Maybe there's a scientist at the university that knows.

Andy: Aren't there some scientists that mainly study insects?

Teacher: Yes, there are. In fact, they have a special name. Scientists who study insects are called "entomologists." Here's how it looks (*I write "entomologist" on the chart*). You can try it. . . . (*Kids practice saying entomologist.*)

Teacher: So how could we track down an entomologist?

Sean: My next door neighbor works at the university. I could ask him if he knows any entimi . . . scientists that study insects.

Teacher: Great! Any other ideas about how we can go about this?

Debbie: We could call up the university and ask who to talk to.

Teacher: So tomorrow we have three different ways that we can try to find out more about cricket eyes. What are those ways? Susan?

Susan: We can do more observations and look more closely, or call up someone . . .

Teacher: Yes. And the last way?

Nicky: We can do research in books.

Extending the initial observations children make at the science table is important (Figure 6–5). It's part of science; it helps children develop their interest and competence; and it's fun. In this meeting I tried to show the children that there was a puzzle to be solved. Observations about the number of eyes on a cricket differed, and I called attention to that difference. Then Claudia pointed out another problem. We were all making assumptions that our observations alone could not support. Pointing out a puzzle or helping children frame a question is the first step in extending work. Then we need to help children figure out how

| **Figure 6–5** | **Drawing of a cricket by girl, age 7** |

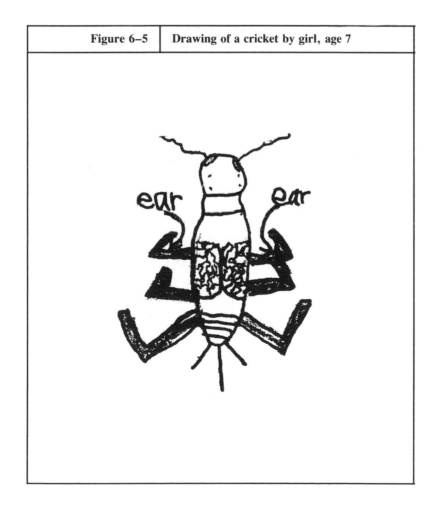

to work on the question. Where can you find information? What kind of people can help? What kind of books? How do you take a closer look? Of course, the teacher will need to stay involved as each avenue is explored. Children will need help learning to use a phone book, dealing with being put on "hold," and trying to state their questions clearly to the stranger on the other end of the line. They'll need help as they learn to focus the microscope, use an index, or skim over a chapter looking for the information that will further their work.

Breaking Down a Big Job into Manageable Steps

A class of seven- and eight-year-olds spent part of a spring morning bird watching in a marsh. On the trip home one of the drivers motioned for our caravan of cars to pull over. A huge bird had perched on a tree near the road (Figure 6–6). We all stopped to watch it for a few minutes.

"What is it?" the children in my car wanted to know.

"It's so big!"

"I think it's a hawk," one child ventured.

"Try to get a really good look at it," I suggested. "If we can remember how it looks, then maybe we can find out what it is." We watched as the bird took to the air and disappeared.

Back at school the children burst through the classroom door. Their excited chatter revolved around the big bird.

"That bird was huge!"

"The biggest bird I ever saw!"

"Did you see it fly?"

"It had to be a hawk. I just know it was."

We had been using field guides occasionally for our bird research and several children rushed to the bookshelf for them. The section on hawks was easy enough to find, but the children became puzzled when they started to compare pictures. The different species looked so much alike! I called everyone to the rug for a meeting. The field guides were distributed so that every three or four children could share one. I pulled over the chart stand and uncapped a marker.

Teacher: First, tell me what you saw when you looked at that bird.
(I record as children speak.)

Steven: It was big!

Janice: It had brown on the back and wings.

Marianne: It had spots on its breast.

Richie: The breast was kind of whitish.

Scott: It looked as if it had an *X* on its chest!

Figure 6–6	Drawing of a hawk by eight-year-old boy

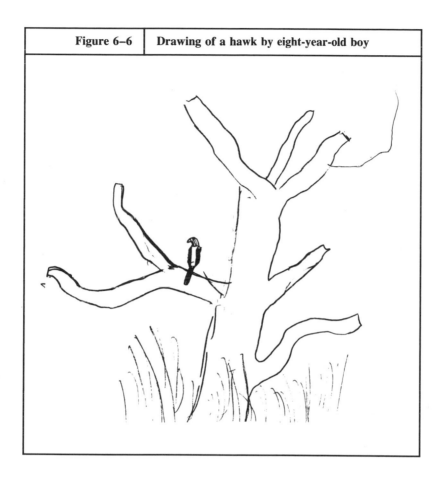

George: When it flew, I could see the wings were big.

Cathy: They were wide!

Eric: It kind of glided.

Audrey: Its tail was orangy on the top.

Jill: The tail was like a fan.

Tony: And big!

Teacher: You remember lots of things about the way this bird looked! And some of you already have an idea about what kind of bird it might be.

Several children: A hawk!

Teacher: A hawk. And what did you see that tells you it might be a hawk?

Steven: It was so big.

Eric: The gliding.

Meg: I've seen other hawks, and it looked like the ones I've seen.

Teacher: So the gliding and size and the way it looks make you think it's a hawk. There are lots of different kinds of hawks. If we just start looking through the field guides at all the hawk pictures to find the one that looks most like ours, it could take a long time. And it could be confusing. But it turns out that there are a number of big groups of hawks—six of them. If we can figure out which of the big groups our hawk fits into, then we'll have an easier time identifying it. The guides tell about the different groups. Their names are: kites, accipiters, buteos, eagles, ospreys, and falcons. (*The children find the page describing these groups and try out some of the names.*) I'll read the description for hawks in the kite group. ''Graceful birds of prey of southern distribution . . .''

Lee: Can't be!

Teacher: Why not?

Lee: Well, we saw our hawk in Deerfield. That's not southern!

Teacher: Okay, then we can rule out the kite group. Let's try the next group—the accipiters. ''Long tailed woodland hawks with short, rounded wings.''
(*The children study a silhouette of an accipiter in their field guides.*)

Cathy: The tail seems kind of too long.

Joey: And our hawk had a fat tail, remember?

Jill: Like a fan.

Teacher: So you're not so sure about our hawk fitting in with the accipiters. Well, the next group is called the buteos, or buzzard hawks. ''Large thick-set hawks with broad wings and wide rounded tails . . .''
(*There are nods, murmurs, and exclamations of ''That sounds like it!'' I quickly read the descriptions of the remaining groups, but all the children agree that the hawk we've seen fits the description of buteos best.*)

Teacher: Now we're ready to take a look at the different kinds, or species, of buteos. Do you see any pictures in the section on buteos that look like they might be the bird we saw?

Marianne: This one. (*She points to a picture of a red-shouldered hawk.*)

Teacher: A red-shouldered hawk. Let's look at the field marks and compare them with the list of things you noticed about our hawk. This guide says that young red-shouldered hawks have dark streaks on a light breast. Did our bird have that?

Children: Yes.

Teacher: And they have dark bands across the tail. Did our bird?

Tom: No. It had an orangish tail.

> (*We check the other birds that look like our hawk. We rule out the ferrugenous hawk because its range does not include Massachusetts, where we live, and the broad-winged hawk because it has stripes on the tail that our hawk lacked. Next we try the red-tailed hawk.*)

Teacher: One field mark of the red-tailed hawk is a "rufous tail" —that means reddish-brown, or orangish.

Charles: Ours had an orange tail!

Teacher: How about "large size"?

Tony: Definitely!

Teacher: Light breast with a band of streaks across the belly?

Audrey: Yes.

Scott: The *X*.

Teacher: All of the field marks seem to fit, so let's check the range. The map in my field guide shows that red-tailed hawks are year-round residents in Massachusetts.

Children: Then that's it!

Teacher: How many people think our bird was a red-tailed hawk?

> (*Every hand goes up. I add mine, and we break for lunch.*)

Part of what happened during our hawk sighting was that children learned the name of a bird they had seen and were wondering about. But more than that occurred. Children proceeded through a set of steps that enabled them to use their observations to make an identification. I set up the steps through my questions and directions to the group.

The first step was to list everything we could remember about the bird we had seen. Next we compared our list with the descriptions for each of the major groups of hawks. We ruled out any groups that didn't match up with our observations, narrowing down our options until we were left with the one that fit best. Eliminating possibilities is an important part of identification, and I try to help children understand that even though they may not always come up with a positive identification, each time they are able to narrow the list of possibilities they have accomplished something. In the last step, we compared descriptions of individual species of hawks with our list of observations.

In this particular situation I took charge of determining what steps to take, guiding the children with my questions. Over time the children will learn to ask themselves these questions, internalizing a procedure that will help them whenever they set to work on a problem involving identification.

Helping Children to Define a Focus

Sometimes children are interested in a topic and eager to get to work, but they flounder when they try to establish the specifics of their research. Perhaps their topic is so broad, or their experience so limited that they are unable to come up with a question they are able to investigate. Or the topic might lend itself to more abstract or sophisticated work than they can manage, and they cannot find a way to approach it that is concrete enough for them to understand. This was the situation with Brad and Jason, two nine-year-old boys.

Brad and Jason came to school one day, excited about the events of the previous afternoon. In the course of playing, they had mixed baking soda and vinegar together, and now they wanted to repeat the experiment so the whole class could watch the mixture fizz. While searching for a container, they discovered some plastic tubes with stoppers. They rushed over to me when they saw these.

Brad: Look what we found! Is it okay if we put the vinegar and baking soda in one of these?

Teacher: What do you think will happen?

Brad: Well, the baking soda and vinegar will start to fizz . . .

Jason (*With an impish grin*): And the top will blow off!

Teacher: And you'd like to see that happen! Well, let's see if we can figure out a way to try it that would be safe.[2]

The boys came up with two solutions. The first was to cork the filled tube and leave it on its side in the sink so that any "explosion" would be contained. The second was to hold the tube champagne-bottle style so the cork would fly up towards some overhanging cupboards (rather than toward lights, windows, or faces). They were delighted when their experiment turned out as predicted, and they demonstrated it for the rest of the class.

During the following week Brad and Jason repeated their experiment many times (mostly on the playground during recess). However, after a few days I could see that the repetition of this work was not holding their interest as it once had. I suggested a meeting.

Teacher: You were right that baking soda and vinegar fizz when they're mixed together, and you've shown how that reaction can pop the cork out of a test tube. What would you like to try next?

Brad: Well, we don't really know.

[2]In retrospect, waiting to try the experiment until we had purchased safety glasses would have been wise.

Teacher: Is this something you want to keep working on, or do you want to switch to another project?

Jason: We like this! We're just not sure what to do next.

Teacher: Here are a few possibilities. You can think them over and let me know if you want to try one. One thing you might want to do is to try to find out if any other chemicals react like baking soda and vinegar. We'd have to figure out how to do it safely. Some chemicals just fizz when you mix them together, but others can be really dangerous!

Brad: We already found out one other thing that fizzes: baking powder and vinegar.

Teacher: So you've made a start.

Jason: Alka-Seltzer fizzes, too. That's how we got started.

Brad: Isn't it because there's an acid and a base or something in it?

Teacher: Acids and bases are two important groups of chemicals. Another project you could do is find out more about acids and bases: what they are, what they can do. Still another possibility is to try to get this reaction you know about to do some work for you. Once I saw a really neat machine. It was a waterwheel that was powered when the gas from fizzing baking soda and vinegar pushed some water out of a container and onto a waterwheel. Maybe you could invent a machine that is driven by vinegar and baking soda power, or a vehicle that can move.

The next day, they returned with a project in mind.

Jason: We're going to make a rocket.

Teacher: Neat! Do you have an idea about how you'll build it?

Jason: Well, kind of. We'll use one of these tubes. But we don't know what else.

Teacher: Look around on the project shelves and see what you can find. When you have an idea of how you want to go about it, sketch out a plan and bring it to me.

Brad: What do you mean, a plan?

Teacher: Remember when we made birdfeeders? Kids drew a picture of how the finished birdfeeder would look, and listed the materials and steps they thought they would follow. Your rocket might not turn out exactly like your plan, but I do want to see some kind of a plan (Figure 6–7).

After a few days of construction with plastic tubes, styrofoam meat trays, masking tape and marker caps, the boys were ready to try their rocket.

I watched from the window. There were a few false starts which

Figure 6–7	Jason's baking soda and vinegar–powered rocket

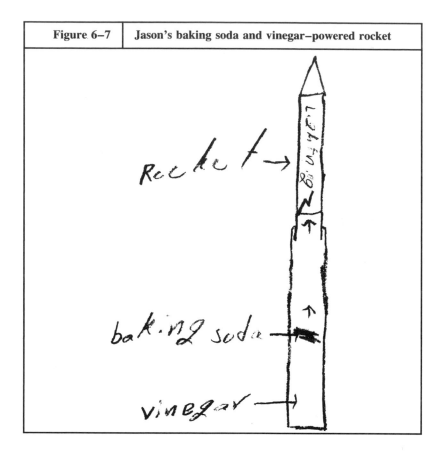

left the ground crew muttering and shaking vinegar off their hands, and then they succeeded in getting the rocket to lift off. It reached a height of a foot or two before it splashed down on the playground.

They returned to the room excited and full of ideas for how to improve their rocket's performance.

Jason: The baking soda and vinegar mix too fast. They start fizzing before we can get the top on, then it doesn't go very high.

Brad: We have to keep them separate.

Over the next week or so, the rocket was rebuilt several times. Another child joined the team, and the second generation of rockets popped up to a height of four to six feet. The boys again approached me:

"Now we want to try a car!"

I watched for a few days and noticed work on the car was not proceeding in a very directed way. I again suggested a meeting.

Jason: We don't really want to do the car idea. It's pretty much the same as a rocket, it just goes sideways instead of up.

Teacher: What about another kind of research?

Brad: Yeah, like that acids and bases idea.

Teacher: What do you know about acids and bases?

Not surprisingly, it turned out that their conception of acids and bases was inaccurate and vague. But their interest was strong, and they began a new project (testing for acids and bases) with enthusiasm.

Even when children have a broad or ill-defined interest, or an interest in a very complicated topic, they can investigate some aspect of it if they are helped to define their focus more narrowly and given some concrete examples of appropriate starting places.

Dealing with Problems and Ethical Issues

One year, a group of seven-and eight-year-olds were studying birds. After just a few days of work on this theme, all kinds of objects began to arrive at school. Several children brought in books with beautiful photographs of birds from around the world. Others brought in field guides. There were records, feathers, and, of course, nests. I quickly became concerned about the nests. They were fascinating to look at and compare, but I was worried that enthusiastic collectors might unwittingly take nests that were still in use. I also felt our class should make collections of any kind thoughtfully, with regard for the environment as well as classroom needs. A few children were disturbed as well. I had overheard a few remarks about the "shoulds" and "shouldn'ts" of nest collecting.

I decided to bring up the issue at meeting. "During the week," I began, "lots of us have been observing all of the different nests that have been brought in for our science table. You've been able to figure out some of the things they are made out of and have ideas about what kinds of birds might have made them. Does anybody know what birds do with their nests?" Many hands went up.

Teacher: David?

David: Their nests are kind of like their houses.

Roxann: Like we have houses, birds have nests.
   (*Many children nod agreement.*)

Teacher: So lots of you think a bird's nest is its house?
   (*More children nod.*)

Teacher: Well, if that's true, what things would a bird use its nest for?

Carol: To sleep in.

Jim: To keep warm in.
   (*I list ideas as they come up.*)

Maria: Then we shouldn't be taking all these nests! Because winter is coming, and the birds will need them to keep warm.

Matthew: But the birds are migrating now! I don't think they use their nests in the winter. I think it's just in the spring for their eggs and babies.

Heated discussion began on this point. If birds used their nests for keeping warm in the winter, the children agreed we shouldn't collect them.

I wrote "Birds use their nests for:" at the top of a new sheet of chart paper, and under it I listed the various ideas that had been suggested.

Teacher: These are our hypotheses, our ideas about what birds do. In order to decide what to do about nest collecting, what do we need to do?

Barb: Find out what one is true.

Teacher: How can we find out?

There were many ideas, and we decided to halt nest collecting temporarily while we did some research.

The meeting that follows came at the end of a week of research. Children who wanted to try to find out more about nests read books, made phone calls, talked to parents and neighbors, and recalled their own observations.

Teacher: Yesterday, Matthew told me that some of you have figured out a lot about—

Matthew (*interrupting*): Yes! About the nests.

Teacher: —while some others of us were away on a field trip, so why don't we make sure that everyone is up to date? The first step is I want to look back over the ideas, or hypotheses, we had about bird nests. Someone can try and read the first one that's up here on the chart. And why did I write it like this— hypothe*ses* instead of hypothe*sis*?

Jim: Oh! Because we have a few of them.

Teacher: We have a few hypotheses and this is how you write the word when you have a few.

Matthew (*reading from chart*): Birds use their nests to stay in in the winter and keep warm.

Teacher: Okay. That was hypothesis number one. Number two, Jamie.

Jamie: Birds only use their nests to lay eggs and raise their babies.

Teacher: Number three, Brendan.

Brendan: Different birds do different things.

Teacher: And number four, Anne.

Anne: Some birds leave their nests in the winter but come back the next spring to the same nest.

Maria: Some birds do 'cause we have a bird at our house that does that!

Teacher: You do! Well, these are the four hypotheses. I know that I went to the pond and looked at ducks for the afternoon, but that a lot of you were back here investigating in books and with phone calls, helping each other get more information about how birds use their nests. Did anybody find out anything about the first idea—that birds use their nests to stay in in the winter and keep warm? Howie, what did you find out?

Howie: Well, I didn't really find out anything but we called and he said he didn't know. You know, Dr. Davis.

Teacher: Umhm. And what was the question you asked Dr. Davis when you called?

Howie: Do birds use their nests in winter to stay warm?

Teacher: So Dr. Davis didn't know if they got in their nests to stay warm or not.

Matthew: A few of us called.

Teacher: And you asked some different questions?

Kids: Yes.

Teacher: Johnnie, what was the question you asked?

Johnnie: Well, I said, "Do birds use their nests in the beginning and then go back for a few years?" and he said that some do and some don't.

Teacher: So you talked to Dr. Davis about if birds leave their nests in the winter, and maybe migrate, like David was talking about, will they come back to the same nest again?

Johnnie (*nods*): And some do and some don't.

Teacher: Did he tell you any way we could know which? We could look in some of those books, I guess. Maria?

Maria: I asked him if birds usually mate in the winter and he said no, birds usually mate in the spring, 'cause they usually would hatch their eggs around summer time.

Teacher: So he said, birds usually mate in the spring and hatch eggs around summer. So they'd be raising their babies in the summer?

Maria: Yeah.

Teacher: Any other research or calls to report on?

Daniel: No, but I just have something to say. I think if birds just leave their nests, do they just stand on their feet all the time or fly?
(*His tone conveys the feeling that this is a ridiculous idea.*)

Teacher: You mean for the winter?

Daniel: Yes.

Teacher: Well, that was the question that Jim and Howie were asking at first. They said, ''What would they do, just stand out there on a branch all winter? That would be ridiculous!'' And then they got to thinking about it more and it seemed to them that maybe that's what birds do. So that's one of the things that we're trying to find out.

Abe: Maria says they mate in the spring and have babies near summer. Then the babies would grow up and have to make a new place to live. So you'd think maybe the babies would go make a nest.

Johnnie: Yeah, after a few months, the parents leave them at a pond or something, wherever they like. I know that because at our pond, just before we drained it, we had some ducks—wild ducks—come, and we saw some parents, and they had babies, and they left them. For a few days they didn't come back.

Teacher: Hang on to that observation for a bit, Johnnie. Maybe these ideas about the babies are part of our next question. What will the babies do if they are going to stay? Kate?

Kate: I asked him about if once the babies leave, do they ever see their parents again. And he said it depends on what kind of bird it was and I asked if they do see their parents again, would they recognize them?

Teacher: Uhuh. And he said . . .

Kate: He told me that they don't know. If they saw their parents again, it depended on the kind of bird, and if they would recognize them. I doubt they would.

Jean: So some might see their parents but not know it's their parents? That's weird!

Teacher: Hard to imagine, huh? So they might see each other again but not recognize each other.

Jean: Imagine just seeing your parents for three months or something.

Teacher: Three months and then . . .

Jean: And then you might see them again but you don't recognize them!
(*Kids laugh.*)

Teacher: Pretty different than us, huh?

Abe: Hi, mom.

Brendan: Like you might be thinking in your head "Where are my parents" and they're right next to you.

Teacher: Well, that's an interesting idea. It might even be that birds think in a different way than we do. That's a question some people might want to start to work on. Any other results of research from yesterday that should go up here?

Maria: This isn't really some research, but I'm trying to figure out how birds act compared to us.

Teacher: Compared to us, good question to research.

Gary: There are too many questions already!

Teacher: We do have a lot of questions! Tell you what. Here's the stuff we found out from yesterday. What it sounds like Maria and Howie have in mind is their very next question, which is just what happens a lot when you start to do this kind of research. You find out the answer to one part of your question and it just gives you another question! Maria is saying that now that Kate has told her that birds may not recognize their parents, she's starting to wonder what other ways birds and people are different.
So I'm going to put up a list of questions and when you have one, you can write it down. And some of them we'll work on all together as a class, and some of them you'll work on on your own or in a small group.

Abe: Do you just write them down on that paper?

Teacher: Yes. Now why were we so interested in finding out about this yesterday?

Suzi: So that we'd know what to do about the nests.

Teacher: Yes. So now we have a decision to make, and the decision is what?

Abe: If you can take them or you can't take them.

Teacher: Our class has to make a decision about if we're going to keep on collecting nests, or not. What was the Audubon Society's decision? When Matthew called, what did they say?

Suzi: They said that you could, as long as you didn't see a bird.

Teacher: That's right.

Maria: But you could have an odd situation, because if the mother or father was just off getting food, it's really complicated!

Teacher: It is really complicated! One of the things you have to decide is if you think that the Audubon Society's rules are the rules that we should go by in our class, or if we want to make up different rules based on what we know. One of the things you just brought up is, if Gabe is there watching the nest and doesn't see any birds, but the parents are just around the corner looking for food, he could take the nest and then, that would be bad for the birds. Dr. Davis says he doesn't know if any birds use their nest in the winter, so that means what?

David: We really have to do some more research.

Teacher: Do we want to go collecting nests when we don't know?

Children: No! No!

Daniel: 'Cause then we might be, some birds might use their nests in the winter. They'd come back and their nest would be gone.

Teacher: And then there's also this thing David brought out. Some do, some don't. You called Dr. Davis and you asked him about it and he said . . .

David: That's it. Some do, some don't.

Teacher: And what does that make you think, Chris?

Chris: Then some might want to use their nest again, but if you take it they can't.

Teacher: Okay. I'm going to take suggestions for our nest-collecting policy. What's a policy? We're going to have one here, so you should know what it is.

Barb: I think it's . . . I'm not sure.

Teacher: Some stores have check-cashing policies. Or return policies.

Barb: Oh yeah, that you can do it.

Teacher: Yes. It's kind of what the rules are about, cashing a check or returning something. Maybe you can return a pair of jeans as long as you didn't put them in the washer and dryer already and shrink them.

Suzi: Or you can return it if it's still in the box.

Teacher: This nest-collecting policy we're going to make up is for now. When we find out more we may have to change it. But I'm taking suggestions for what goes into our policy for right now. Roxi, got an idea?

Roxann: You can only take a nest if you're sure the bird isn't going to come back to it.

Teacher: And how could we be sure no bird is coming back?

Roxann: Because you could watch it. If in the spring no birds come, then you can take it.

Johnnie: Baltimore orioles don't come back to their nests.

Teacher: Okay. Sounds like there are two ways. What was the way Roxann suggested you could find out?

Jody: By watching it.

Teacher: Yes, and if in the spring, no birds come back, after you've been watching it all winter, then it's likely no one's using it. And what's the way Johnnie suggested?

Johnnie: Baltimore orioles never use the same nest again. So if you find one in the fall, you know you can take it.

Teacher: Okay. Any other additions to the policy?

Abe: It's not really an addition, but remember, Marlynn said her brother took down a nest, and the birds did come back, but they just built another one.

Marlynn: Yeah.

Teacher: So that can happen, too. What do you think that means?

Abe: It might be that all birds do that, or it might depend on the kind of bird it is.

Teacher: So would you agree that we should leave a nest unless we're sure it's not going to be used again?

Abe: Yes, but if we could find out what kind of bird that was, we could look in a book.

Maria: I still don't think it would be fair to take it, even if they can build another nest.

Teacher: And why is that, Maria?

Maria: Because they might have liked their old nest better.

Jonas: No! No!

Teacher: Leslie?

Leslie: Well, like if you took their old nest and they came back and built another one they might still be looking for the same old nest.

Teacher: So, do you want to leave your policy saying, "You need to be sure that a nest is not going to be used again before you can collect it?"

Children: Yes.

Teacher: And you just heard two good ways to try to find out. Are there any ways to collect nests if you see one that you're really excited about but you can't figure out for sure if a bird might come back to it? Is there another way to collect without bringing it into the classroom?

Suzi: We could go on a field trip to see it.

Teacher: Okay. You could invite the class on a field trip!

Barb: You could do an observation of it.

Roxann: You could take a picture.

Gary: You could just share about it.

Jean: Talk about it.

Marlynn: You could look in a book and see if you can find a picture of it and then show the class the picture (Figure 6–8).

An important, but too often neglected, aspect of science teaching involves dealing with values and ethics. Opportunities for this are many. The instructions that come with our incubator tell us that by opening one egg every few days, we can directly observe the dramatic changes in the developing chicken embryo. However, this procedure will kill the embryo as well as allow for observation. What do we want to do? Later, when the chicks hatch, the children will want to hold and cuddle

Figure 6–8	**Nest Collecting Policy**

Nest Collecting Policy

You need to be sure a nest isn't going to be used again before you collect it. There are ways to study or "collect" a nest without taking it. You can:

arrang a field trip

do an observation

take a photo

share about it at meeting

do research on it

them every minute. How much handling is good for a baby chick? A spotted salamander is brought to school one early spring. The children are fascinated by this seldom-seen animal and want to keep and study it. However, it has been collected in the middle of its brief breeding season—what should we do?

I want to help children realize the connections between themselves and the world around them. I want them to develop an awareness of their impact that is appropriate for their age and to make decisions about their science work that conform to their values. Similarly, I need to consider my own values in making decisions and, at times, establish classroom policy myself in line with those values. For example, I decided that children who had learned to handle classroom pets could take them out and handle them in many areas of the room, but not in the loft and the block area. Children might argue this decision: "But at home we make mazes for our guinea pig to go in and the blocks never fall" or "I want to take Checkers up into the loft so I can read him a story. It's better up in the loft so we want to do it there." These are situations I'm not prepared to allow, no matter how great the value of direct experience. The consequences for both the pets and children if blocks tumble or an animal is dropped on the way up the loft ladder are serious, and I'm not willing to risk them. Whenever I do have such a "bottom line" I try to make it clear, and also share my thinking with the children. Children are able to disagree with my reasoning, but as the teacher I will make the final decision. Fortunately most situations that come up have a variety of solutions that are acceptable. I believe it is important for children to be given the chance to think, discuss, and create classroom policies that reflect their values and concerns.

Dealing with such issues can be time consuming. In the preceding example, the class worked for a week, meeting, researching, thinking, and discussing, before the nest-collecting policy was developed. However, when we hurry on with our science projects, glossing over concerns or ignoring the consequences of our actions, we say to children that it does not matter what effect our work has on the world around us, that scientists pursuing questions that interest them do not need to bother about such things. When we take the time to consider our values and how our actions relate to them, we say to children that it is important to be responsible and considerate—in both our classroom and the world.

7

Interpreting Children's Work

Classroom teachers are continually planning and evaluating, deciding from one moment to the next which direction to steer the class and how best to help individual children. We base these decisions on knowledge we gather while watching the children, interacting with them, and reviewing their products. The following pages offer a closer look at some of the ways to gather and use information from children's work.

I have begun with samples of worksheets, written and illustrated by children aged five through eleven, because they demonstrate some interesting aspects of how individual children approach science at different ages. From each worksheet we gain insight into one child's ideas, accomplishments, and priorities. The worksheets have been annotated to highlight some of the observations that are reflected in the drawings and to translate "invented spellings." I have also commented on some of the characteristics that typify children's work at different ages, focusing on developmental changes that can influence the way teachers plan science activities, form expectations, and interpret children's products.

Teachers who are unfamiliar with children's representations or are used to editing or correcting children's products may feel unsure of how to respond when a child proudly presents a completed worksheet. Looking over the work, we may see careful attention to detail, but also errors and omissions. The emphasis on accuracy and objectivity that we have come to associate with science may make us especially aware of "mistakes."

I do not grade or correct these worksheets, but I do discuss them with children. It is validating and helpful to children when teachers

111

can reflect some of what they see in a child's drawing or writing. Comment on what is there, rather than what is not there ("You discovered how a cricket chirps!" is helpful; "Your cricket had four legs? Look again—all insects have six legs" is not).

In order to appreciate children's work, we must learn to see what they are showing us. You may wish to cover up the captions that accompany these worksheets in order to practice looking at and identifying important aspects of the work.

Many times we want to see children extend the work they have begun. After commenting on something we have noticed about their observations, we may choose to ask them questions that will encourage additional research. Since the way we pose questions indicates our acceptance or our disapproval, it may be useful to try to imagine what "next step" might be fruitful for the child who did each of these worksheets, and to think of how to respond to each in a way that is likely to encourage further investigation and interest.

Danny's guinea pig observation

Danny (age five years, seven months) has captured the oblong shape of the guinea pig's body. He has included a head and four legs and has shown that the guinea pig has no tail. Within the body Danny has drawn the heart, stomach, and liver (parts he cannot see, but explained, "are on the inside"). The lines of the guinea pig's head have become a decoration around the page. Children at this age sometimes mix designs, fantastic colors, and smiling faces with actually observed details. The legs of Danny's guinea pig don't quite connect to the body. Though many five-year-olds would not leave such a gap, some will.

Danny's writing reflects his understanding that lots of letters can be used to express an idea; however, he has not used letters that relate to his verbal description of what he has noticed.

Danny had chances to look at and hold the guinea pig prior to this observation, which probably contributed to his ability to focus on drawing and writing. He was also able to talk informally with classmates as he worked, an aid in thinking about the guinea pig. This is an important time for children to be gathering experience and developing language to describe their world. Teachers responding to these discussions do well to remember that young children's explanations and reasoning about causes and effects will reflect their immaturity.

Figure 7–1	Danny's guinea pig observation

Name of Scientist **Danny**

I looked at

A picture of what I saw

I noticed HE DVRAN

Mandy's guinea pig observation

Mandy (six years, eight months) has shown the shape of the guinea pig's body and head with more accuracy than a younger child would. She has also included many details, such as short legs, feet with toes, a black eye, a pink rounded ear, the pattern of brown and white fur, and a mouth and nostril. Six-year-olds' drawings tend to be more detailed and realistic than those made at five, but happy faces and decorations are sometimes still included.

Mandy has scribbled brown fur and quickly outlined and partially filled in the log in the guinea pig's cage. This "dashed-off" quality is common at her age.

Mandy has written, "It eats the log. He jumps." These statements describe the most notable behaviors of the guinea pig during this session. On an earlier worksheet, Mandy also included her reactions to the animal: "He is cute. I like him." Mandy's writing, like that of many six-year-olds, combines capital and lowercase letters, invented and conventional spellings, and letter reversals. I accepted these without comment since they occur in the writings of many young children and will be outgrown in time.

Figure 7–2	Mandy's guinea pig

Name of Scientist   **Mandy**

I looked at   eUinea PigS

— A picture of what I saw —

I noticed   IT eATS The
LAG.
~~XXXX~~ he TaP.

Rita's cricket observation

Rita (seven years, eight months) has made a small, detailed drawing of a cricket after erasing an even smaller first attempt to its lower left. She has worked entirely in pencil rather than in color. Some children prefer pencil, perhaps because of their interest in precision.

Her drawing shows the front and hind legs of the cricket, jointed and angled. She has also included abdominal segments, several other divisions on the body, mouth parts, two taillike cerci, and two antennae originating near the eye.

Rita has written: "It had four legs and two little things up in front that it ate with. It had little lines on its bottom, and it chirped for me and I looked and saw little wings moving." It is evident from both her drawing and her discovery of how a cricket eats and chirps that she has devoted considerable time and attention to this observation. Rita is well on her way to becoming a cricket expert. With her increasing mental capabilities, she is ready to organize and interpret information in new ways. Now that she has discovered how a cricket chirps, she might consider whether all crickets chirp, or just some. She might be able to determine whether all chirping crickets chirp the same way, or if individuals have variations. With a teacher's help, she will be able to think of many other possible areas of investigation. At this age some children become so engrossed in their amassing of details, they lose direction. Rita's teacher will need to help her organize an approach and maintain perspective.

Figure 7–3	Rita's cricket

Rita's observation

date: August, 29th, 1988,

I looked at A criket.

A picture of what I saw

Here are some things I noticed:
it had 4 legs and to little things up in front that it ate with.
it had littlle lines on it's bottom.
and it chirped for me and I looked and saw little wings moveing.

Ray's spice finch observation

This drawing by Ray (age eight years, six months) shows the spice finch perched in its food dish, with front toes over the edge and back toe opposing the front. Wing, tail, and head are shaded brown; the breast is covered with tiny brown markings. The fat beak on this bird is a characteristic Ray and his classmates have come to associate with birds in the finch family. Ray's picture exhibits his developing capacity to create realistic drawings with close attention to detail. Combining art and science offers Ray opportunities for both experimentation and focused instruction in art.

Ray has written: "I noticed a pattern about the finches. That I think the male goes out and eats some food then either gets a piece of grass and goes back in or he just goes back in." Identifying patterns is important in understanding bird behavior and in other science work as well. Ray's spontaneous identification of a pattern provides an excellent point of departure for further, focused observation. At this age he can design and carry out simple investigations, keep records, and use reference books with more independence than he could at seven (although he still needs a teacher's help in organizing and carrying out a project).

Ray has taken care to use the term "male," rather than "father," when referring to the finch.

Often parents and teachers become concerned about spelling and punctuation as children grow older. Ray has generalized the use of apostrophes, writing "go's", "git's," and "ete's." Although this would be a good skill to work on in a separate exercise, creating a focus on apostrophes here might detract from his important observation of a pattern of behavior.

Figure 7–4	Ray's spice finch

Ray's

observation

date: 5/4/88

I looked at SPISE finchis

A picture of what I saw

Here are some things I noticed:

I notist a Patar abowt The finchis That I Thing The Male Go's Out and ete's som food Than ethor Git's a pase of Gras and Go's Bake in or He Jost Go's Bake in.

Susan's nest observation

Susan (age nine years, two months) has drawn a nest built into a forking branch. She has blended colored pencils to show the shade of the nest and tree bark. Rather than attempting a literal depiction of each leaf, she has sketched in green and brown lines to give the effect of many leaves.

Her writing reflects the different senses she has employed while exploring the nest, as well as her curious observation: "It is strange how the leaves stayed green and they are dry." It is as if her observation has contradicted her preconceptions about dry leaves. Susan has already amassed a wealth of information about the world from her own experience, from books, and television. Applying this information to new situations and testing what she has heard and read against her own direct observations are processes to encourage.

Susan is quite capable of extending her work and designing an investigation that might lead her to learn more about her surprising observation. She could compare the leaves in this nest with other dry leaves or experiment with drying some fresh leaves and note changes. Continuing to observe this nest over time, focusing on any changes in the color of the dry leaves or in the "fresh" smell, would also help her develop her understanding.

In categorizing an observation as "strange," Susan has taken the first step towards raising a question to research. She will also be able to conduct simple investigations of her own design. Though a teacher may perceive "holes" in her procedures or reasoning, she will learn from solving problems as they arise.

Figure 7–5	**Susan's nest observation**

Susan's observation

date: Feb. 26, 1987

I looked at a nest

___ A picture of what I saw ___

Here are some things I noticed:
it is soft it smells fresh it
is strange how the leaves stayed
green and ~~still~~ they are dry. it
has alot of detail it has birch
bark and pine neetles and
sticks. it is pretty small.

Ethan's finch observation

Ethan's worksheet reflects attention both to the appearance and behavior of the finches. In his drawing this ten-year-old boy has used lines to suggest feathers, and he has given the birds humanlike eyes. He has shown both birds in profile (erasing a first attempt to draw the finch in the nest basket—face on). Many children find ''sideviews'' of animals easiest to manage. Ethan's drawing suggests interaction and activity.

In observing ''that the top of the head goes right to the beak without going down,'' Ethan has discovered for himself a characteristic that distinguishes finches from many other birds. Aspects of nesting behavior have also been noted both in his illustration and his writing. ''One is usually in the nest, the nest has a lot of grass in it, I think that they're going to have babies soon.''

Ethan could extend this research in several directions. He could classify the birds he knows according to some observable feature, such as beak shape. Activities involving sorting, classification, and listing information are enjoyed by many children his age. He could also explore the bird's behavior further. (Do the birds take turns in the nest, or does one bird do most of the sitting? Do the birds select any other materials besides grass for the nest?) Since children reveal many of their ideas on these worksheets, teachers may often find the worksheets useful springboards for discussions. Ethan's prediction that the birds are going to have babies, for example, might lead to an interesting discussion.

The study of bird behavior lends itself well to field work. Though fieldwork is important and enjoyable at any age, many older children seem to thrive on it. They are energetic, capable of keeping track of equipment (with occasional reminders), and often enjoy being outside for extended periods. Ethan and his classmates spent quite a bit of time observing birds out-of-doors.

Figure 7–6	Ethan's finch

Ethan's observation

date: 5/13/88

I looked at The finch's

A picture of what I saw

Here are some things I noticed:
I noticed that the top of
the head goes right to
the beat with out going
down, one is usually in the
nest, the nest has alot of
grass in it, I think that their
going to have baby's soon

Susan's turtle shell observation

Susan (age eleven years, one month) has made a drawing that shows the color of the turtle shell, the arrangement of the different "pieces," and a pattern or design on each piece. She has used quotation marks to differentiate between words that are generally accepted terminology and a less conventional word she has used ("jags"); she has also drawn a diagram to ensure that her readers understand her use of this term. Her description of the turtle shell indicates a thorough examination of the inside, the outside, the individual parts, and the object as a whole.

Although her drawing does not perfectly replicate the pattern on the turtle's shell, her observations will enable her to begin the process of identification. Susan has included a discovery that may not be of importance to scientists generally, but certainly was striking to her: "The piece that came off the shell looks like the U.S. of A. with a shrunken Florida and no Cape Cod!"

From her previous experience with turtles, she has correctly concluded that the end where the "jags" arise is the front. Many children will include such information to enrich their observations.

The little curves she has noticed are a kind of "growth ring." Following up her observation with some reading could lead to some exciting connections. Many children at this age make excellent use of appropriate reference books. As children's thinking matures, the investigations and research they are able to tackle becomes more sophisticated.

Though Susan was comfortable using a familiar worksheet for her record keeping, teachers of older children may want to change the format of worksheets or meetings so that work will not be perceived as "babyish." Children can often design the record-keeping systems best suited to their purposes. For an example of Susan's work at age nine, see Figure 7–5.

Figure 7–7	Susan's turtle shell observation

Susan's observation

date: 1/18/89

I looked at One of the turtle shells.
and some of the pieces from the shells,

A picture of what I saw

Here are some things I noticed:
The shell has the spine of the turtle on the inside,
there are "jags" rising up from the shell:
in the front (where the turtle's head would be)
it is raised up. The piece that came off the
shell looks like the U.S. of A. with a shrunken
florida and no cape cod! The brown parts
have lots of little curves.

Children with Special Needs

Science work can be interesting, fun, and exciting for all children. Throughout this book, children with special needs have been shown observing, experimenting, and discussing ideas with teachers and class-mates, raising questions and searching for answers. It was Carrie in chapter 1 who approached me as I cleaned up pieces of a broken bottle saying, "I was wondering, maybe we could make sea glass," and Alex in chapter 2 who taught himself to draw guinea pigs by studying a classmate's picture. Ricky and Patrick in chapter 6 sifted through a bag of potting soil to see if they could find support for their hypothesis about the origin of the weeds that had appeared in their tulip pots, and Angie discovered the circular ears on a frog, later involving her class-mates in figuring out how a frog's tongue works. Maria was the first student to raise concerns about nest collecting. Her own observations of a nest in her yard (occupied by birds year after year) prompted her concern. And it was Maria who recognized the difficulty of determining whether or not a nest with no bird in it had truly been abandoned: "But you could have an odd situation, because if the mother or father was just off getting food, it's really complicated!" The care and attention Phillip devoted to recording twig observations (see Figure 7–15 later in this chapter) inspired similar attention and care from many class-mates.

Diversity within a classroom is a valuable asset, especially when children work together on science. Many observations contribute to our growing store of information. Many skills enable us to identify and pursue questions, solve problems, and express understanding. When science work is broad and varied, children (including those with special needs) have the greatest opportunity to grow and to contribute to the growth of others. I am struck by how often the child who struggles with writing can reveal a wealth of interest and information through her drawing, movement, or music. Often the child who seems most ill at ease within the confines of the classroom is the very child who emerges as a leader in the field, able to locate the tiniest of wildflowers, make endless trips for firewood and drinking water without tiring, or lend support to a classmate afraid of thunder, darkness, or snakes.

One way to maximize learning opportunities for all children is to provide many avenues for learning and expression at school. It is equally important to provide encouragement and support for children when they attempt work that proves frustrating or difficult, or when they make the inevitable comparisons between their products or abilities and those of classmates. Children with learning disabilities or other special needs can feel confused when trying to follow a class discussion, frustrated when they can't read their own written observations, or concerned about the way their work looks on display. It may be difficult to retrieve the words, facts, or figures that would make their ideas clear to others.

Noel, age nine, told her teacher, "I think my brain is like a rubber ball. The information goes in, but then it just bounces back out." Teachers and classmates can help as children struggle to overcome these difficulties by creating an environment in which each person is treated with respect. In science as well as in other areas of the curriculum, the particular strengths and needs of different children shape their approach and products. There are many ways to work at the science table, keep records, or contribute at meetings.

Some Ideas for Individualizing Science Work for Children with Special Needs

Sustaining observation. Many children have difficulty focusing their attention during a work period at the science table. They may look briefly at the object on display, then get up and move to another activity; they may look out the window instead of at the object provided for observation; or they may be easily distracted by activity elsewhere in the room. Looking closely, the first step of the observation process, will challenge these children. It may help them if the teacher can define "observe" even more specifically than she did during the whole class meeting. "Observe means you look closely. When a scientist looks closely at an object, she looks at the top, and the bottom, and at the sides—all around! A scientist looking at this shell would even have to look at the inside! When you've had a good look at all of the parts of this shell—its top, bottom, and sides—then you'll be ready to start your drawing."

Initially, a teacher can be available to make sure that children both understand what it means to look closely and are able to do it. Later, a checklist can be provided so that children can monitor their own work.

Other aspects of observation work may also need to be defined very specifically. "A good description of an animal tells at least three things about how it looks. One thing you can look for is color. What colors do you see on this caterpillar?"

Not all children will be able to sustain an observation or work on a drawing or description for the same amount of time. One seven-year-old may work for forty minutes. Another may have trouble focusing for five. Defining and limiting a task helps some children who have a tendency to "flit." By providing them with specific things to look for and report on at the science table and a checklist or other system to let them know when they are done, we enable children to work with greater independence and do work of a higher quality, extending their ability to participate in the class.

Record keeping. Records can be written by the child, or a teacher or classmate can take dictation. Any system that allows information to be remembered and shared is a good one.

When children do tackle their own record keeping, there are many ways to make their task more manageable. When repeated observations are made of the same subject, checklists can simplify recording information. Children can work with teachers to develop forms. (For example, the class can list or draw pictures of bird behaviors; an observer can cross out or check those seen.)

Words or phrases that have come up as the class discusses observations can be listed on a chart or written on index cards fastened together with a metal ring. These can be posted or stored at the science table, available for children to copy. Children without special needs often benefit when labels or charts containing relevant vocabulary are displayed. Building up and making available a controlled vocabulary for children who struggle with writing is especially important.

Individualizing expectations for written work is also important. Some eight-year-olds will easily manage a two-page report about their crickets; others will have to work hard to manage one sentence. Teachers need to match children's assignments to their abilities. Some children who have difficulty with written or spoken language express themselves more readily through drawing. When they find that drawing is viewed as a legitimate and valued means of sharing information, they are more able to focus on drawing as a means of expression. For these children, writing tasks can be kept to a minimum; drawing and other means of recording or communicating can be emphasized. At times, tape recording children's observations may be useful. Again, any system that allows information to be remembered and shared is a good one.

Sharing worksheets. During meetings, teachers can help children who are unable to read their own writing by providing tape recordings or special notations. Children can also talk about their ideas and observations without having to read from their worksheets. Rehearsing by reading a worksheet prior to a meeting helps some children. A teacher can also supply a child with sentence patterns to make written or spoken language more manageable.

Teachers can help children recall or articulate ideas and discoveries by prompting or pulling out ideas the child is having difficulties expressing at a meeting. Assisting children with the job of recall or retrieval can simplify sharing for some students. For example:

Teacher: I remember, Paul, that when you were looking at that blue feather the other day, you noticed something unusual about it. Remember when you held it up to the light? What happened?

Paul: I don't remember.

Teacher: It was the color . . .

Paul: It changed!

Teacher: You showed me how the color changes from blue to brown.

Sometimes a child's oral delivery of information is confusing to classmates. This can be embarrassing and frustrating for both speaker and listeners. A teacher can often come to the rescue restating ideas in a way that enables the child to communicate more clearly and enables classmates to appreciate the student's good thinking. The teacher's choice of words at such a juncture is important. The teacher's language must clarify what the child has expressed in a way that credits, rather than corrects. The following example from a bird-watching trip illustrates this:

Carol: We saw those—you know—not the ducks but the other ones.

Teacher: You saw the geese?

Carol: Yes. We saw the geese, and when that man put the food out, they were eating it, but not the ducks. They just stood there. But after, we saw the ducks eating. I was thinking maybe they have to wait. The other ones go first.

Teacher: I see! Your idea is that when it's time to eat, the geese eat first. When the geese are finished, the ducks can take a turn.

Carol: Yes. Like they're the bosses.

Teacher: The geese are the bosses.

When we recognize and help children express what they know as this teacher did with nine-year-old Carol, we enable them to contribute at meetings and we ease the embarrassment and frustration that otherwise might occur.

Emphasis. When many kinds of contributions are valued, children have lots of different ways to be successful. If a teacher or class focuses too intensely on a particular aspect of work (for example, the quantity of written work or the realistic appearance of drawings), many children may feel frustrated or inadequate.

The following worksheets were completed by children with special needs who participated in all aspects of the science programs in their classrooms. At the time, they were receiving ongoing services that addressed the special needs that had been identified by teachers and evaluators. The age of each child is given together with a description of individual special needs.

Seth's twig observation

Seth (age six years and three months and grouped with five- and six-year-olds) is a child with significant fine motor difficulties. He finds writing and drawing tasks difficult. Here he has observed a twig and shown the pattern of its branches and the jar that held the twig. He chose a brown pencil to indicate the color of the bark. Seth was able to observe and discuss orally far more than he could convey on a worksheet, so informal discussions with a classmate or teacher were an important part of his science time.

It was also important to give Seth time to observe without having to produce a worksheet. Seth's teacher alternated between taking dictation and recording one of his observations for him, having Seth record his own observations, and asking Seth to draw his observations without writing.

Figure 7–8	Seth's twig

Name of scientist **Seth**

I looked at my twig

I noticed It was

brown.

Bruce's spice finch observation

Bruce (age nine years and one month; grouped with seven- and eight-year-olds) struggles with comprehensive language difficulties that affect his reading, spelling, and ability to organize his thoughts in speech or writing. On this worksheet he began recording his observations in the usual place, but moved to the top of the sheet when he ran out of room at the bottom. He placed the word ''finches'' directly above his picture rather than on the lines provided above it.

Bruce has drawn both finches in their nest basket. Each has a beak, wings, and eyes, and the bird on the left has lines to indicate feathers.

Bruce has written, ''One of the finch's stomach is getting big and that one is staying in all the time and both of them are in there now. They are making walls for the nest . . .'' (words just under the picture are unclear). The nesting behavior of these finches held Bruce's attention longer than usual and resulted in quite a bit of writing. A checklist or a teacher's reminder to use pencil instead of marker and a finger space between each word could have helped him record his interesting observations more legibly. Bruce's observation of both finches on the nest at once was added to a class list of new finch behaviors. Such a list could be used to help build a controlled vocabulary for the science table.

| Figure 7–9 | Bruce's spice finch |

Bruce's observation

date: _____

I looked at _thayo— maina_
wols for tne he
_st_ A picture of what I saw _fethes_

Here are some things I noticed _befret, and the_
Luv the fen her in a
stumck is atime
beg and that liste
in gin ol the tiny
and botnur tnum
lor in tnurnaow

Kurt's salamander observation

Kurt (age eight years and eight months; grouped with seven-year-olds) works to overcome visual-perceptual problems that affect reading and spelling. Note *d-b* reversals. He has written, ''It has a line down its back and orange and black spots. It has an eye.'' Kurt's drawing is an exceptional likeness of the salamander. Colors are blended to show the orange skin, and shading along the ''line down its back'' gives a three-dimensional look. Leg configuration and other details are also accurate. Drawing is an important mode of expression for this child and a strength he can share with his classmates.

Figure 7–10	Kurt's salamander

Kurt's observation

date: _____

I looked at _a___Salmaner.___

_____A picture of what I saw_____

Here are some things I noticed:
It Has a line dawe Its
dack. and Aringg and dlak spos.
It Hase a heye.

Mitch's robin mount observation

Mitch (age nine years and one month; grouped with seven- and eight-year-olds) has struggled with oral and written expression. Word retrieval and sustaining attention are difficult.

Mitch put considerable effort into his drawing of the robin mount, erasing several attempts before he was satisfied with the shape he had drawn. He has shown the long narrow bill, the wing reaching up over the back, and the toes curved around a perch. Colors and markings are basically accurate. Mitch has written, ''Its tummy—brick red. It has a little white. They only have black eyes. It has black fingernails. It has grey on its back. It has ugly feet. It eats cherries. 8½ inches.'' His description focuses first in great detail on the bird's colors. Mitch also included some information about size and diet read to him from a book. Specific language from the book helped him to complete his description—''brick red'' for the reddish-orange color he noticed on the breast, and ''cherries'' as part of its diet.

Figure 7–11	Mitch's robin mount

Mitch's observation

date: Sept 24 1985

I looked at^ robin mont

_____ A picture of what I saw _____

Here are some things I noticed:
it's tame brikred it has a
liettile with they on lie have black
eys It has black fagernels It has
grey on it baek It has ogle feet
it^ cheares 8kinch is

Maria's feather observation

Maria (age nine years and ten months; grouped with seven- and eight-year-olds) works to overcome both auditory and visual difficulties. Her academic skills are more than two years delayed. Expressing herself verbally and sustaining attention are also difficult for her. Maria has observed a great horned owl feather. Both her investment in this project and her artistic ability are evident in her drawing, especially in the way she carefully blended colors to show the feather's markings. She has also written about the pattern: ''I noticed it is brown and black on one side and on the top on the other side, brown, yellow, and brown lines. It has black [and] brown lines on it.''

There was a marked discrepancy in the quality of Maria's observations on worksheets and during class discussions. Although she had to struggle to find the words to explain her ideas, she was quick to make connections during a discussion or put observations to use during a field trip. The gap between written expression and understanding can create problems for some children; teachers need to develop expectations that are appropriate for each child and provide ample opportunity for investigation without always requiring a worksheet component.

Figure 7–12	Maria's feather

<u>Maria's</u> observation

date: <u>Mar. 4 1988</u>

I looked at <u>a fra</u>

_____ A picture of what I saw _____

Here are some things I noticed:
I ~~aome~~ noticed it is brown
and Black on one side and or
the top on the of side brow
yollon and lan browii, It have Bai
brown sns lans on It.

Allison's guinea pig observation

Allison (age eleven; grouped with nine- and ten-year-olds) struggles to understand things she hears. She finds conversations, spoken directions, and lectures confusing. Putting her own thoughts into words is far easier. Art is an area of real ability. Her drawing of the guinea pig is accurate and detailed—pink, folded ears, and fur sticking up along his back and head. She has carefully included the other details of the scene in front of her as well, drawing each plant on the windowsill, the can and the log in the guinea pig's cage and even water dripping from the water bottle. Allison has written, ''I noticed that it looks like it was blown with a hair dryer for an hour. It has white and brown fur. And little feet that have toenails like needles.'' This descriptive imagery and the inclusion of the entire scene before her in her drawing often marks her work. When science work is not too narrowly defined, there is room for varied interpretations of a task. Children can draw on different strengths and contribute individual perspectives.

Figure 7–13	Allison's guinea pig

Allison's _____ observation

date: _____

I looked at _a Ginny pig_____

_____ A picture of what I saw _____

Here are some things I noticed:
I noticed that it lookes like it wos
blone with a hare drier for a
awer. it has white and brawn
fer.
And little feet that have
toanails like needle's.

Evaluating Children's Work

If we are committed to a curriculum that has curiosity and independent thinking as goals for children, we may need to discard more than a preprogrammed textbook approach to teaching; we may also need to discard familiar ways of evaluating children's progress. Chapter tests may measure student progress in a program where the goal is to master facts, but they communicate little about a child's ability to observe, ask questions, or pursue ideas. By developing alternative strategies for evaluating and reporting that avoid ranking children or passing judgment on their ideas, we can sustain the spirit of cooperation and collegiality that is so essential in the classroom and we can encourage independent inquiry and experimentation.

The Purpose of Evaluation

The purpose of evaluation is to increase our understanding of the children in our classroom so that we can make informed decisions about the particular approaches or opportunities that will benefit them and communicate with parents or other teachers about their work.

To expand our understanding of children, we must examine them across many dimensions, observing the way they approach their work as well as the products they create. In science this means paying attention to what children do when they observe at the science table, play in sand, share information at meetings, or resolve their own questions. It also means studying the drawings, writings, and constructions children make to represent their discoveries and knowing what these products communicate. We use evaluation to learn how a particular child approaches activities and what generates interest or difficulty. This understanding is what we summarize and share with parents at conference time and what we use to guide our daily decision making and planning in the classroom.

An Approach to Evaluation

In the kind of evaluation I am discussing, the teacher gathers information from three sources: informal observations, formal observations, and product files.

Informal Observations. Teachers make continual "informal" observations of children throughout the day. A teacher might take mental note of specific behaviors or form general impressions while leading a science meeting, helping a child use reference materials, or watching as children cuddle the guinea pig. In the beginning of the year I find that informal observations reveal many things about a child's development, interests, priorities, abilities, and style of working.

Often, we can put this information to immediate use. We can offer help to a child who appears confused or encourage a child exclaiming over a discovery to explore further. We may also store these impressions in our files so that we can refer to them as the year progresses.

Formal Observations. During "formal" or planned observations, teachers observe and record the activities of individual children, as they work alone or in groups, focusing on particular aspects of their behavior. I generally sit near the children I want to observe, notebook in hand, sometimes interacting with them to probe their thoughts or observe specific behaviors and other times keeping silent so as not to influence their actions. Each method yields important but different information that will form part of the written record for each child.

Formal observations often grow out of informal ones. In our daily work with children, we may be puzzled or intrigued by something and decide to schedule additional time to examine it in more detail. We may also schedule time for observing at particular junctures, making sure we look at each child in relation to specific goals we have set.

For example, one year I labeled "raising questions" as an important goal in science. I wanted children to be able to pose questions of their own, rather than respond only to the questions of others. Since the information I gathered through informal observations did not always allow me to know whether or not children initiated their own questions, I decided to look at their questioning skills in a more formal way. The need for formal observation also arose with Miles and Cory, the two seven-year-olds in chapter 2 who spent so much of their time at the science table looking at crickets. My impression was that they were interested in the crickets, pursuing research of their own design, but this impression could have been incomplete or inaccurate. To verify that their conversations at the science table were indeed about crickets, I again relied on formal observation.

Product Files. Teachers can keep a file of each child's products (sample worksheets, photographs, or descriptions of models or other constructions, copies of reports and other writings) collected at regular intervals throughout the year. When we are able to review a collection of products made over time, we often notice patterns or changes in a child's work that might escape us if we looked at products individually, sending each home soon after its completion.

The file also helps us see progress and accomplishments. Allison, a seven-year-old child with a learning disability, began the year carefully recording her observations with detailed drawings, but made no attempt to write. In March she drew a bird brought in by a classmate; underneath she wrote "I think it looks very pretty." At the end of April she filled her worksheet with a detailed description of two baby snapping turtles.

Sometimes we observe things that cause us concern or prompt us to work with a child on a specific issue. Eight-year-old Jeremy handed in an observation of a large bone. "It has bumps," he wrote. "It's neat."

An occasional description of this quality would not have aroused my concern, but my impression was (and the product file verified) that "It's neat" appeared on Jeremy's worksheets at least as frequently as the more detailed observations I expected. I needed to review my expectations for Jeremy and consider possible strategies for helping him to take a step forward.

Product files also may reveal something about a child's approach to work—a particular interest, or ability, or style. Peter observed an owl feather (Figure 7–14), reporting: "On the dark side there are seven stripes. On the light side there are eight stripes." Later, he counted up the number of plates on a box turtle's shell. Another time he recorded the number of teeth in a jawbone. Noticing number seemed to be a frequent self-chosen focus of his.

Reviewing a child's product file can deepen our understanding of that child and aid us as we plan further work. Children may also keep files of their own, using them in the classroom both as reference books and records of their growth.

Some Thoughts About Grading

Many teachers have asked what criteria to use when grading observation work. I avoid assigning letter grades or adjectives (for example, "excellent," "good," "fair," "poor") to rate work. In addition, I recommend against "correcting" errors in spelling, grammar, or terminology.

Though grading may be necessary at times, I am against it here for a number of reasons. One reason is that grading seems unrelated to the purpose of the work. In science we want children to draw and write because the process helps them to observe more carefully and the product helps them remember discoveries and share those discoveries with others.

If we want children to make full use of the learning opportunities afforded by drawing, writing, or modeling, we need to free them from the burden of having an outside judge assign a value to their work. If, in the process of drawing a cricket, a boy trying to fit the wings onto the body notices that there are not just two but *four* wings, then important scientific work has been done. If, on his final product we note the cricket has no antennae or eyes or comment upon his hastily written sentence about "wings in two kinds" and we give him a B −, or even a C, we devalue his self-directed inquiry and the resulting discovery. Or, at the least, we create a new focus on the grade that counters our emphasis on interest, exploration, and experimentation.

Grading has other drawbacks. By establishing ourselves as the

Figure 7–14	**Peter's feather**

Peter's   observation

date: 3/3/88

I looked at _a_ _Grat hothd OWl_
feather

_____ A picture of what I saw _____

Here are some things I noticed:
oh own sid of the feather
it is litt than thee.othr,
oh: the dark sid that are
suvin strips oh the lit
sid that are aet sthips.
oh the lit sid the feathr
is fosy all the way up
the ohiyi ofht sid has fos oh the bctow

judges of children's products, the ones who know good from bad, we encourage children to rely on us to evaluate their efforts. But work in science requires some independence, the ability to interpret findings, and a willingness to make choices about what to pursue. I want children to build an independent sense of purpose and standards rather than rely on me to determine the worth of their work. Further, grading encourages children to compare their work in a competitive, rather than a cooperative, way. Since I want children to draw on each other as resources, discuss findings, and learn from each other, I want to avoid labeling work in a way that might cause children to feel they don't need input from others, or have little to offer. There is also the danger that grading will encourage children to see science as a discipline in which there are clear-cut right and wrong answers and to imagine that their job, during investigations, is to produce the right answer, which the teacher surely has.

Some Thoughts About Standards

Abandoning grading does not mean abandoning standards or a dedication to high-quality work. There are many ways that teachers can help children develop high standards and grow in their work.

One March, I took a class of five- and six-year-olds for a walk. In a vacant lot behind a grocery store we looked at different trees and shrubs, still dormant after a New England winter, and collected twigs to bring back to our warm classroom. The plan was to put the twigs in water and observe them for several weeks, noting changes and recording observations.

The children were very excited about the project. They loved twisting their tongues around the word "botanists"—the word I had introduced to describe us during this phase of our science work—and each happily decorated a label to identify the jar that held his or her very own twigs. Some children even collected extra twigs so that they could "watch one at home."

The children's cheerful attitude continued throughout our first scheduled observation period, but not mine. Looking around the room, I saw children approaching their work with chatter and haste—looking quickly, drawing quickly, and announcing "I'm done." As they hurried to put their observation worksheets in folders or on the bulletin board, I looked over the drawings. There were purple, blue, and pale pink twigs. There were budless twigs, branchless twigs, and twigs that looked like porcupines. Though I knew that at this age a certain enthusiastic speediness was to be expected, I also felt that these children were capable of more care and attention than I had seen. I had hoped to see them looking more closely, discovering the tiny features and patterns that made each twig unique, recording their ideas with more realism. After a second, similar session I puzzled over how I could encourage more careful attention without sacrificing the happy enthusiasm.

Before our third observation session, I brought in two books to share at meeting time. Both were beautifully illustrated books about plants. One had dozens of color plates depicting North American wildflowers; the other had delicate line drawings of aquatic plants.

Teacher: I brought these special books to show you because I know that you are interested in your botany work. Some botanists, like you, study twigs and trees. Other botanists study different kinds of plants. Can you tell what the botanist who wrote this book was studying?

Denise: Flowers!

Teacher: Yes. This whole book is about the wildflowers that grow in this country. Just as you are observing and drawing your twigs, the botanist who made this book observed flowers and made pictures to show people how they look.

Eddie: And they wrote about them.

Teacher: And they wrote about them, too. I'm going to show you a picture from this book. (*I turn to a color plate of violets, flowers I think the children will recognize. Immediately hands go up.*)

Connie: Oooh!

Phillip: We have those at my house!

Amanda: They're violets!

Jon: That's a good picture!

Lorna: I have lots of those!

Ray: Yeah—they're violets.

Teacher: You're right! This is a picture of violets. How could you tell?

Phillip: 'Cause they're just like the ones at my house.

Teacher: Artists can make all kinds of pictures. But the artist that made this picture of a violet for this wildflower book was trying to show people something particular. This is a science drawing and the artist wanted to show people . . .

Shelly: How it really looks.

Teacher: Yes. What things about this picture are like a real violet?

Pat: The color—the flowers are purple.

Kenny: Not only purple. In the middle there's a tiny bit of white.

Amanda: I've seen that!

Teacher: Yes—purple with a tiny bit of white, just like real violets. Anything else?

Eddie: The leaves!

Teacher: What about the leaves?

Eddie: They're green.

Anne: There's lots of them.

Sandy: They go like this (*shows them bending*).
(*We look together at a few more color pictures of wildflowers, the children identifying what makes each painting look realistic. We also examine several of the line drawings of aquatic plants. Even without color, these drawings are beautiful as well as realistic.*)

Teacher: What makes this a good scientific illustration?

Kenny: They worked so *carefully.*

Teacher: How can you tell?

Kenny: Well, they didn't go out of the lines.

Teacher: These books are here for you to look at. When you go to do your botany work today, you can think about the things you will want to show about your twig. What can you use if you want to show the colors?

Micky: Crayons.

Linda: Colored pencils.

Teacher: Yes. And what different parts do your twigs have that you could show?

Suzanne: Buds.

Dale: Little branches.

Brent: Mine is red.

At the next scheduled observation time I sensed a change in the tone of the room. There was still a happy eagerness among the botanists, still a few spills as children hurried to get their jars and worksheets, but once settled, their pace relaxed a bit. I circulated among the children, commenting on the detail and realism I saw: "I notice you made lots of branches in your drawing, Connie, just as your twig has lots of branches"; "I see you drew the forked shape of your twig, Pat."

A few children called me over to share a discovery. "I noticed that the buds on my twig are side-by-side—in pairs," Lorna pointed out. I moved in for a closer look. "Yes. I see that they are! I wonder if all twigs have buds in pairs or just some twigs, like yours?"

I was struck by a dramatic change in the work of a few children. Phillip had been settled and focused for almost fifteen minutes, a striking change from last session's early "I'm done!"

His drawing, too, had changed enormously. Before, two purple sticks with no distinguishing features rested in wavy lines of water. This time Phillip had shown two parallel rows of dark buds, green leaves just unfurling, and reddish-brown bark (Figure 7–15).

"Phillip!" I exclaimed, "You have shown so much about your twig in this picture!"

"I had to use all these crayons," he explained, indicating a wide array of colors, "because when I looked at my twig, I could see lots of different colors on it."

At our science meeting the next day, Phillip shared his drawing

Figure 7–15A	Phillip's twig: First drawing

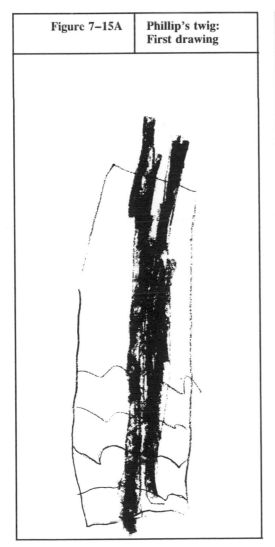

Figure 7–15B	Phillip's twig: Second drawing

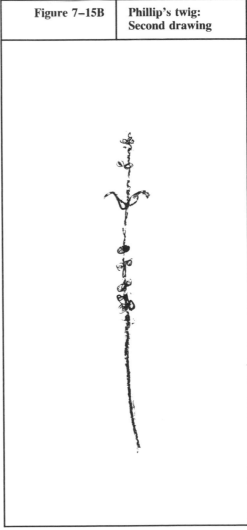

with the class. I held up his twig for comparison. "I noticed that the bark has lots of colors," he read. "I'm ready for questions and comments."

"I like your picture," one child stated.

"It's good," nodded another.

"It is a good scientific illustration," I agreed. "What makes a science drawing a good one?"

"If it looks like the real thing," contributed Ethan.

"What can you see on Phillip's real twig that he showed in his drawing?"

"The bud."

"Different colors."

"Those two tiny leaves."

"All those things tell us about Phillip's twig," I agreed.

At our next observation session I again felt a change. Children settled quickly to work and commented often to workmates as they noted particular aspects of each twig. As children called me to see their finished drawing and writing I noticed that "I'm done" had been largely replaced by other kinds of announcements. "See? I made the buds in pairs, the way they are on my twig." "Guess what? My twig has tiny leaves and they are sticky on the bottom!"

Of course, each child progressed with this work in an individual way. Amanda continued to draw her twigs with an extraordinary number of branches, but she showed the relative sizes of her specimens and sometimes showed the color of the leaves and buds. Dennis still checked the room to see that he was among the first finished, but wrote about a change he had noticed and often lingered to watch another child work. Betsy designed a system for tracking changes, comparing the twig to her previous drawing before she began.

I think of quality work in science as being marked by attention and care, a willingness to put forth an idea and consider another's idea, and a willingness to add to or revise an understanding or product to reflect new observations (keeping in mind, of course, that six-year-olds and ten-year-olds deliver very different care and attention).

Teachers can provide children at any age with the opportunity to work toward appropriately high standards, instead of establishing one standard that all children must meet. Teachers can also help children look critically at their own products and ways of working, identifying the ingredients of "good work" and supporting children as they attempt to change.

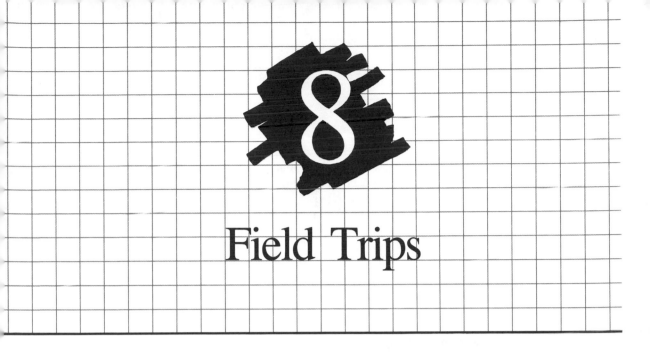

8

Field Trips

Knowing that the weeks between the end of spring vacation and the beginning of summer could be difficult ones, a fourth-grade teacher planned a day-long trip to a science museum in a nearby city. She hoped that a special trip would help pull the class together by giving them an exciting experience to share and new ideas to bring back to the classroom. She arranged for bus transportation and chaperones, and the museum sent a map of the exhibit halls and a schedule of special demonstrations along with the confirmation slip. The opportunity for a break from the daily routine, access to specimens and equipment not available at school, and a knowledgeable museum staff to answer questions excited everyone.

On the morning of the trip, children, lunches, cameras, and chaperones were loaded onto the bus. After unloading and checking in at the museum's main desk, the teacher pointed the way to a part of the building housing large-scale physical science exhibits, many of them interactive. The children exploded down the corridor, delighted with the echoes created by their loud voices and pounding feet. One group discovered a giant wave tank and pushed the button that set it in motion. They watched for a second, then pounced on another button that caused a strobe light to flash on a falling stream of water. Both exhibits continued to operate as the children's attention was caught by a large funnel suspended by chains; sand dripped from it and formed patterns in a large box below. The children took turns pushing the funnel toward one another and catching it, before racing across the hall to another room where they had noticed a computer. In the computer room, two chaperones sat on a bench, discussing weekend plans. Nearby a group of girls giggled as they worked to maintain their position midway up the escalator, running down toward the first floor as the moving stairs rose towards the second. Midmorning, the class was entertained as a museum staff member demonstrated the effect of liquid nitrogen on flowers, rubber balls, and spinach leaves. Many children were amazed by the display; others bombarded their teacher with repeated requests: "Can we go to the gift shop now?"; "Can we do the gift shop as soon as this is over?"; "When will it be time for lunch?"

The bus ride home lasted an eternity. There were squabbles over where to sit, loud conversations about scary movies, louder complaints about the loud conversations, and Nathan's special rock from the gift shop fell while he was showing it around and rolled under a seat where no one was able to find it. Afterwards, the teacher wondered whether she would ever take the children out of the classroom again.

Most of us have had an experience something like this and have struggled to understand what it was that went wrong. In discussing field trips with other teachers, I find there is much agreement about the value of fieldwork:

"There are such wonderful resources in our community! A university, a natural history museum, a small nature preserve. I think field trips can really enrich a classroom program."

"It's exciting for the kids to get to go somewhere new."

"I want them to learn about the environment. You can't just learn about trees from looking at leaves and bark in the classroom, or by reading. You have to go see a real, live tree!"

There is also much agreement about the difficulty of such work:

"The kids just go wild! I have to be on top of them every minute."

"When you take thirty kids out of the classroom, you really need to be able to count on the chaperones to help out. Sometimes I have more trouble with the chaperones than the kids."

"My kids are wonderful in the classroom. But last month, when we went on a trip to a local greenhouse, I was really surprised by their behavior! They were rude, actually wandering off when our tour guide was speaking, interrupting, fooling around. The guide wasn't used to children, I don't think; he tended to talk "over their heads." But they could at least have been polite!"

Work outside of the classroom (whether it is a trip to the far side of the playground to hunt for ants, or a major expedition to a museum in another town) can be a very special part of elementary school science. Successful field trips are exciting, contribute to classroom work, and demand a great deal from children and teachers!

In the classroom, children can come to rely on predictable routines and boundaries. Outside of the classroom, though, many familiar routines and boundaries disappear. Without them, some children become anxious. Some wonder if class rules have vanished along with the desks, chairs, and daily schedule. Some children may be reluctant to leave their teacher's side; others are all too eager to move out and investigate this new area, experimenting to see just what limits are in place!

Teachers, too, can feel uncertain when they move with children beyond the familiarity of the classroom. They may worry about particular children. ("When Davy's activity level starts getting out of hand, I usually suggest he work at the sand table or with clay. Those activities seem to calm him. What will I do with him at the bird sanctuary?") Roles may also feel unclear when other people (tour guides, naturalists, or program instructors) step in to teach the class. We can do many things to help ourselves, chaperones, and children work productively out of the classroom.

Understanding About Work in a New Situation

Some years ago, when I was an instructor at a large science museum, I came across an article about field trips, which presented the results of research about children's ability to learn in novel settings and in more familiar ones. During a class's first visit to a nature center, the amount of learning (related to teacher-staff objectives) was fairly low. On subsequent visits to the same center, learning increased. After many visits (when the setting had perhaps become "too familiar"), interest and learning began to wane. At the time, this article gave me some insight into the behavior of school children visiting the museum where I worked. It was commonplace to see flocks of children spiraling down the central staircase, spraying into the lobby below like so many pinballs, or to be in the midst of a talk about the live owl on my shoulder and be interrupted, not by a remark about its interesting behavior, but with the question "Where does that door over there go?" or "How big is this place, anyway?" I continue to reflect on this work from my present situation as a classroom teacher.

In a new situation, many children need to devote lots of energy and attention to exploring their surroundings, locating themselves, figuring out what to do and how to act. For some children this is a scary business; others adjust fairly easily. In either case, while children are busy with the work of exploring, locating, and adjusting behavior, they will have little ability to focus on the pattern of waves in the "Giant Ocean Tank," or the differences between white oak trees and red oak trees. When children have grown more accustomed to their new surroundings and are clear about what is expected of them, energy is freed for scientific observation, investigation, or instruction.

In essence, a field trip is not really very different from the first day of school. On that first day, children enter the classroom excited, nervous, wary, or unsure. We could greet them with a lecture about the parts of a flower or send them to work experimenting with household chemicals—but most of us don't. Instead, we offer time to explore the room, learn the names of classmates, find the coatroom, the bathroom, the playground. Field trips require an adjustment to a new setting, too; the trouble is, we don't have a whole school year to grow comfortable working in this new setting. Following are some techniques and ways of thinking that can help field trips work.

Start Small

Many schools have limited funds available for buses and the many other expenses associated with field trips. So teachers may plan just one or two trips a year, and these are major events. Children and teachers are required to cope with enormous and instant changes (a new place, new rules, new adults, a long bus ride, and a different schedule) without much prior experience. No wonder difficulties arise! An alternative approach is to start taking field trips early in the year, and to take them often. Make the trips local, short, and simple. One year, when studying birds with seven- and eight-year-olds, our first field trip was a walk around the block. We were bird-watching. Another year, I went with a group of seven- and eight-year-olds to the flower garden at the corner of the school yard to see if we could find any crickets. In yet another year, we went to the office and the furnace room—we didn't even leave the building!

Plan and Model with Children

The science area is opened with deliberation and care, with children helping formulate a definition of what scientists do and practicing various aspects of the work. Field trips need to be introduced just as carefully. I meet with children, and discuss ideas about what fieldwork is, and what fieldworkers do. As with in-classroom work, we proceed from a general definition to talking about and modeling specific jobs and behaviors that will enable us to work. The following example illustrates this process.

Teacher: We are going out to look for birds! How do you think scientists find birds?

Janie: Well, they have to look very carefully. Some birds kind of blend in.

Karin: That's camouflage. Some animals are camouflaged.

Teacher: Where might you look?

Children: Trees.
Bushes.
Some might be flying.
Telephone wires.

Teacher: So we'll have to look in lots of different places. But on our trip, we'll be going past lots of different peoples' houses, and we'll be near some busy streets. Can we just run over to the bird feeders or go stand in the road to get a good look at someone's tree?

Children: No.

Teacher: Who can show how it is we can look different places, but stay together on the sidewalk?

Different children had ideas, and we practiced this part of our fieldwork. We figured out what materials we wanted to take and how we could call the group's attention to birds without making so much noise that we scared them away. By the end of the meeting, children knew that they were going to begin the part of science research called fieldwork, and they had a sense of the specific jobs they would do (Figure 8–1).

Figure 8–1	Drawing made by eight-year-old girl on bird-watching trip

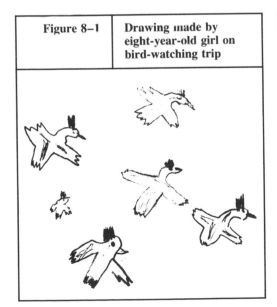

Figure 8–2	Teacher walking with students in crosswalk

Safety

If we are to take children out of the classroom responsibly, we need to feel confident that we can keep the class together and safe (Figure 8–2). Having plenty of adult chaperones along is part of planning for safety and so is knowledge of the particular place we are going (for example, where is the nearest telephone, the drinkable water, the poison ivy). We also need to know that we can count on the children to follow directions, stay with the group, come when we call, and help each other. Before any trip away from school, we teach any special signals or systems we'll be using. I find the same ones I use in the classroom and on the playground are adequate for most trips. If I raise my hand, that means "Freeze and listen." If I say "Circle up," everyone comes to where I am standing and forms a circle. Sometimes each child has a number, or a partner, so that we can "count off" and quickly see if anyone is missing. When I see that children can do these things easily and quickly on the playground or in the classroom, we can leave school grounds. Some science field trips (for example, boat trips, difficult hikes, or overnight camp outs) demand a great deal of responsibility from children. I work to prepare children for these trips—but if the trip date is approaching and I don't feel confident that our safety systems are in place, I postpone or restructure the trip.

Practice

There are many aspects of fieldwork for children to learn. On an actual trip, they will need to do many things at once: focus, observe, listen, question, keep track of materials, keep track of the rest of the class, interrupt their work to gather in a group, listen to new plans or directions. At school, these varied jobs can be taken on and practiced separately. Children need time to practice all the parts of fieldwork, from behaving appropriately on the bus to asking thoughtful questions, from walking with a partner to looking for pond animals. Before trips (and often during trips) we need to take time to practice.

Maintain as Much Stability As Possible

Once children are comfortable with observing and discussing objects at the science table, we can expect them to observe and discuss comfortably in a new setting (the playground, the park, or the woods). By varying just one major condition, we allow children to draw on their experience and competence. If we change the setting, work, rules, and expectations all at once, their job becomes much more difficult. Few children will be able to do what we ask of them on such a field trip. My feeling is that the more novel (or in any way difficult) the new setting is, the more comfortable and familiar the work needs to be. If children are used to bird-watching, or using observation worksheets, we can expect that, after some time exploring a new location, they will be able to focus on observing and recording. In fact, the presence of the familiar structures may be reassuring for some children and help them focus. It would be unrealistic to expect children to be able to learn about their new surroundings and how to bird-watch and record observations all at once.

A teacher I knew worked at a nature camp; school groups attended the camp for week-long sessions during the fall and spring. At this camp, a "night hike" was an important part of the program. Children walked in the woods at night, listened for animals, stargazed, and learned the patterns of some of the easier-to-locate constellations. But before heading for the woods, this teacher sat with the children near

Figure 8–3	Students recording observations in notebooks

the camp buildings, passed out paper and crayons, and let them color. It wasn't very "sciency," perhaps not even very sensible (coloring in the dark), but, as she explained: "It's a big deal, being out in the dark. It's scary, and these kids are only eleven or twelve; they're away from home; they're not used to the woods; and I'm not even their regular teacher! So we color. Everybody knows how to color!"

Simple, concrete things that can help maintain a sense of stability and predictability are bringing class rules along; following lunch, recess, or meeting routines; and using familiar worksheets or work materials (Figure 8–3).

Establish Boundaries

Within the classroom, many familiar boundaries tell children what to do. The classroom walls define a space within which certain things can be expected. When we leave the classroom, we need to establish new boundaries. This is particularly important in places that can feel enormous or frightening to a child (a big woods, the night, or an unfamiliar part of the city). Sometimes we can physically mark or walk off boundaries. Children may like to explore a plot of ground after they've marked its perimeter with string (Figure 8–4), or it might help to hear "You can do your observation anywhere in this field—but you need to stop at the cabin and the tree line."

Sometimes the boundaries have less to do with a particular space and more to do with staying together. On trips, I expect children to stay with the group. For each trip, we need to define and practice whether that means keeping in sight of the teacher, exploring within whistle range, or walking next to a partner on the sidewalk.

Clear Expectations

Children in the classroom need to know what is expected of them. They need to know the teacher's responsibilities, their responsibilities, where there is choice, and where there is not. Out of the classroom, this kind of clarity is equally important, but it may be more difficult to achieve. Collaborating to establish the general purpose, specific work, and any rules for each trip is important.

Teachers can work with parent chaperones, tour guides, and instructors to make roles clear. Chaperones will need to know how to

| Figure 8–4 | Student observing in plot outdoors |

take charge in some situations when the teacher is not available (for instance, when the noise level in the car becomes too loud for safe driving). While we can share our instructional role with a guide, we nevertheless remain in charge of our classes, responsible for tone, discipline, and safety.

Consequences

Clear consequences need to accompany clear expectations. In the classroom, we can discuss our expectations for how children will work together, and what steps we will take when children forget or test rules the class has established. Before we move work out of the classroom, we need to think through not only our expectations, but what assistance we are prepared to give children who struggle with those expectations and what consequences will result if expectations aren't met.

Integrating Field Work and Classroom Work

Field trips that are a part of ongoing classroom work have more meaning than field trips perceived as isolated occurrences. In preparing for a trip, teacher and children need to discuss the connection between fieldwork and classroom work. The fieldwork itself then fuels work in the classroom. We may follow a bird-watching trip with an afternoon of watercolor painting or journal writing, collect pond creatures for further study in the classroom, construct a model, or write a report, a song, or a story using data gathered outdoors.

A Framework For Successful Field Trips

Keep in mind the difference between working in novel and familiar settings.

Start small—with short, simple, local trips.

Plan and model trip with children.

Plan for safety.

Practice "safety systems" and field trip jobs with children.

Maintain as much stability as possible.

Establish boundaries in the new setting.

Establish clear expectations for children's work and behavior, and clear roles for adults.

Anticipate possible difficulties children may have. Be prepared with appropriate help and consequences.

Follow up fieldwork and integrate it with classroom work.

Making Changes

The importance of the teacher in the approach to science I've described cannot be overemphasized. If, as science teachers, we intend to create a classroom environment that fosters active investigation and experimentation, we must first make provisions for our own learning and confidence in the classroom. We can do this by taking the time to learn about the world through firsthand investigation and by taking charge of curriculum decisions. Just as classroom work must begin "where children are," decisions about what aspects of the curriculum to focus on or what and how fast to change must be based on our own interests, experience, and abilities.

Teachers as Scientists

When we are interested in the world around us, our excitement and enthusiasm fuel work in the classroom. If our early science experiences have resulted in continued curiosity and a sense of ourselves as people who can find out about the things we wonder about, we are fortunate. We are already interested and ready to think about ways to share this interest with children. But if our early science experiences have left us feeling that science is confusing, boring, or beyond us, we may have to work to rediscover the interest and ability we think we lack.

Whatever our background, as teachers of science we need to observe, wonder, ponder, take note of patterns, and search for connections. Like the children we teach, we learn as a result of our own activity—our own struggle to make sense of what we see. The ideas about learning that guide our work with children will help us to guide our own learning.

I believe that, to learn, teachers need to explore in the kind of climate I have talked about setting up for children. We need the time and freedom to question and experiment, and we need others who can help us as we search for new understanding. Setting up such an environment for ourselves often proves a great deal more difficult than setting one up for children, but it is an important step to take for our own sakes as well as for the children we teach.

Beginning with Observation

One teacher I know invited parents to come to school in the evening to observe the same pond animals that their children had collected and observed in class. The teacher's directions to the parents were simple.

"Check out this pond water. Find something that interests you and see what you can find out about it. You can write and draw about what you see."

Parents went to work in much the same fashion as their children. They scanned the dishpans of mucky water, rediscovering familiar creatures or locating brand new ones, talking, laughing, sketching, and writing. Some found out how difficult some pond animals are to see (when still, they can blend right into the silty bottom). Others found out how difficult some pond animals are to catch. One parent discovered some tiny red worms; another found a spidery creature with hairy legs; still another noticed the delicate pattern of spots on the slippery olive skin of a tadpole.

One father had a strong background in science. He'd taken many science courses in both college and graduate school in preparation for his career in veterinary medicine. After a long period of observing with fascination the minute creature he had discovered and examined under the microscope, he commented to his child's teacher, "This may be the first time in my education that I've had the chance to figure something out for myself."

Teachers, like these parents, need chances to figure things out for themselves. There is no substitute. One simple way for teachers to begin is by observing in an environment close to home. The following lists may help you get started.

Things to observe

pets

flowers

house plants

trees

vegetables

fabric

insects

other ''bugs''

rocks

shells

the water pipes in your house or apartment

a construction site

birds

different kinds of wood

Questions to start you thinking

What does it look like, feel like, smell like?

Does it have parts?

Does it move, go somewhere?

How can it be distinguished from others?

What is familiar, a surprise, a puzzle?

Getting Help

Some ways of teaching may lead children to think science is dull or inaccessible. Similarly, some people whom we call on for help may reinforce those attitudes in us. Others empower us, renew our interest, or help us to take a step forward. After years of generally noticing birds, I decided that I wanted to know more about them. For a while I tagged along after any knowledgeable birders who would accept my company. What a difference between the ones who ticked off the names of birds as they flitted into the underbrush and the ones who patiently watched alongside me, giving me time to see and sharing something of their own approach to birdwatching.

''These shorebirds are tricky to identify,'' an experienced companion agreed. ''They're all basically brown, leggy, and wading in the mud. So the first thing I try to do is figure out what basic group a bird belongs to—plover, or sandpiper, or whatever. Take a look at that bird to your left. How would you describe its beak?''

We need to seek out the kind of help that allows us to begin at our own level, pursue our own questions, and develop confidence and ability as investigators and teachers. Children need different kinds of help at different times and so do we. The focused help with identifying shorebirds was useful to me only after I'd spent some time on the coast, discovering these birds and my own interest in them, and perceiving enough on my own about their basic differences to lead me to wonder who was who. At an earlier point, when I was still struggling to learn how to locate and focus on a bird with my binoculars, this help would not have been very useful.

Sometimes the kind of help we need is a partner to share in our explorations (Figure 9–1). Sometimes we need a direct answer to a specific question. For many of us, help has come through workshops, special coursework, or friends and fellow teachers with similar interests and goals (Figure 9–2). We can always evaluate the kind of help we are receiving. Help that makes us feel anxious, or stupid, or uninterested in science probably isn't useful. We need to search for help that keeps us going, builds our confidence, and expands our interest in the world.

| Figure 9–1 | Sometimes the kind of help we need is a partner to share our explorations. (Photo by Ken Williams) |

| Figure 9–2 | Teachers at a summer workshop observe and discuss specimens collected on a field trip (Photo by Ken Williams) |

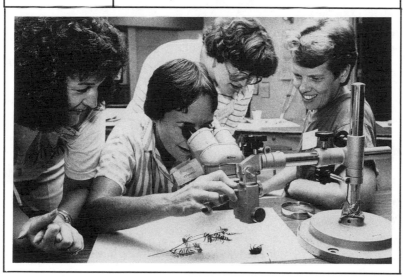

Teachers Extending Observation Work

Marnie, a first-grade teacher, introduced herself at the beginning of a science workshop, explaining, "To me science was just learning specific facts . . . a real bore!" She partnered up with a fellow teacher and began her work, observing a collection of irregularly shaped, hard, white objects. She and her partner carefully described them, drew them (somewhat apologetically), then sorted them into groups by shape. I stopped by to see how things were going.

Marnie: We think they're teeth.

Teacher: What makes you think so?

Marnie: Well—they look like teeth! There's this shiny part, like the enamel on our teeth.

Evelyn: And these long pointy ends could be the roots.

Teacher: So you think they would fit in a mouth this way, with this part showing?

Marnie: Actually—maybe they would go this way, with the points up.

Teacher: Like this?

Evelyn: I don't think that's it. The enamel should be the part that shows.

Teacher: How could you check out your idea?

Evelyn: Look at some things we're sure are teeth?

Marnie: Compare them.

Marnie and Evelyn arrived early for our next session. They added two wisdom teeth (extracted years ago from Marnie) and a small, rootless tooth (donated by a six-year-old) to the collection of objects they had been studying. Their comparisons led them to conclude that they were indeed looking at teeth, and that the shiny part was the crown, visible when the teeth were in the animal's mouth. Closer inspection of the teeth revealed tiny holes at the end of each root ("for the nerves or blood vessels"). The women continued to work and to wonder about several related questions: Just how are teeth lost? What kind of animal lost these teeth?

Evelyn: You know, these look like my cat's teeth. She has long curved ones like this, and pointed, bumpy ones like these others at the back.

Teacher: Do you want to take them home so that you can compare?

By our next session, the whole class was waiting for the tooth report. Evelyn had compared them with the teeth on her pet cat and found many similarities, but enough difference in size and shape to make her doubt that the teeth had belonged to a cat.

Another Participant: What about a dog?

Evelyn: Now that's an idea! (*looking at me*) Do you know?

Teacher: Well, I did find those teeth, so I do know some things about them. Do you want me to tell you what I know now?

Marnie: No! Don't tell! We want to try to figure it out for ourselves first.

Marnie and Evelyn then turned to the school library for help. There were many books about animals, but nothing that really helped with tooth identification. Their work came to a temporary standstill.

Teacher: Maybe there's another way to work on this. You think these things you've been observing are teeth. You've sorted them into several groups based on shape, and you think that all of the different teeth could have come from the same animal. Your cat has several different kinds of teeth and so do we. But although these teeth are similar to a cat's, the match isn't quite right. Who might know about teeth and be able to help you find out more about these?

Marnie (*laughing*): My dentist!

Evelyn: Oh, I know, let's call the vet!

During a lunch break Marnie and Evelyn arranged to bring the teeth to a local veterinarian. The vet confirmed their idea that the objects were teeth, and that they belonged to a carnivorous, or meat-eating, animal, but not one he had seen in his practice.

Marnie: So these teeth aren't from a domestic animal. The next step
would be to take them to a zoo, maybe, or a museum.

Our course ended before a museum trip could be arranged, so Marnie and Evelyn were happy to hear what I knew about the teeth. They were from a seal. Rather than end their investigation with hearing this piece of information, the teachers excitedly left for the library. Now that they knew what kind of animal the teeth were from, those books might be of help after all!

Marnie's own work as an observer and investigator during the workshop led her to conclude:

> Prior to taking this course, I truly thought that science was a real *bore*! To me science was just learning specific facts. However, I now realize that the most important factor concerning science is that the emphasis is on involving the children in the process of observing, questioning, exploring, experimenting, and finding out. I firmly believe that the teaching of science is going to be a *great* experience for me!

Making Changes in How Science Is Taught

Midway through a summer science workshop, I listened as teachers described the classroom situations they would return to in the fall and their thoughts about making changes.

A few were skeptical about the possibility or need for change:

"I just can't see this approach working in my school. There's no support, no materials, nothing."

"It doesn't make sense to spend so much time on one topic. There's a lot of information kids are going to be expected to know when they leave my class."

"All this focus on just how to talk to kids seems overdone. If a rule at meetings is 'no talking' or 'no teasing' or 'don't poke your fingers in the animal's cage,' kids understand that. What difference does it make how you say it?"

Then there were the energetic optimists:

"I can't wait to get back and set up my science area! I'm going to ask my father-in-law to build me a science table. He's helped me with my classroom before. I don't really think there's much special equipment I'll need.''

''I still don't know that much about science but that doesn't really worry me anymore. I'll just learn right along with the kids.

Most of the teachers formed a third group. Committed to goals such as providing children with more opportunities for active exploration or helping children to develop and pursue their own interests, they spoke with frustration about the obstacles that threatened to keep them from bringing their actual science programs closer to these ideals:

''I may be ready to do without a textbook, but I'm not sure my principal or the parents of my students are!''

''The kind of science work we've been doing this week takes lots of time. Kids need their time to 'mess about' and talk to each other and observe, and our schedule is already too full!''

''I had fun finding out about the turtle shell. I can just imagine how much fun it would be for my kids. But I still feel I don't know much about science. I'm not sure I'll be able to help them with their questions.''

Defining Problems, Creating Solutions

As the workshop week continued, teachers discussed their concerns and searched for solutions. Gradually the tone of these discussions began to shift from one of frustration to one of possibility. Perhaps we were influenced by the optimists among us, or maybe it was the decision to focus on just one aspect of teaching at a time, to move forward in small, manageable steps rather than try to change everything at once. Time and discussion may have also influenced us. Whatever the case, teachers began to define specific problems and to create workable solutions.

On Required Textbooks

Problem: ''This textbook I use in my class is eighteen chapters long. The expectation is that we'll get through the whole thing. Many of the units are very broad (the plant kingdom—or weather). I find myself hurrying the kids. I also have questions about the appropriateness of some of the material. We study about marsupials in Australia, but we don't know anything about the animals that live in our own county.''

Solution: ''I'm thinking I might start to use the textbook differently. In the past, I've always started a topic by having the kids 'Open to page 34,' but I *could* start them off with an observation. We could look together at an animal, and the kids could decide what interested them about it. Then we could use the textbook later, kind of like a reference. Or I could just read a chapter at story time. I bet they'd be a lot more excited!

"And I could just let everyone know ahead of time—we aren't going to cover all the chapters this year!"

On Field Trips

Problem: "I'd love to take the kids outside! Our school has the perfect place to explore—a shallow creek at the edge of the playing fields, with woods on one side—but I'm the science teacher for the fourth, fifth, and sixth grades at our school. The kids come for two forty-five-minute periods a week. By the time we got out to the creek, we'd have fifteen minutes to explore before we'd have to turn around and head in again!"

Solution: "Now I'm thinking about how to change the schedule. If I can get the kids' regular teacher to swap a period with me once in a while, I could schedule the kids for two 45-minute periods, back to back. That would give us plenty of time. Or maybe I could sometimes use recess or gym time."

Problem: "Our school has no money for field trips. We can't get bus money to take kids places, even though there are wonderful things to see in our area."

Solution: "I'm wondering if the school yard has the potential for interesting science work. And there are some people who garden in the neighborhood. I'll need to find some extra help—aides or parent volunteers—in order to go on a walking trip with my class of thirty."

On Lack of Knowledge

Problem: "I feel like I don't know enough. It's okay to answer a kid's question with 'I don't know what that is! Let's find out!' if you know how to find out. But lots of times I don't know where to begin."

Solution: "Maybe I need to pick a unit I know something about for starters."

On Materials

Problem: "We don't have any science supplies at our school! No microscopes, magnifying glasses, or specimens. It's hard to run a program with no materials."

Solution: "I realize that lots of the equipment we need kids could bring from home. I wish I had a water table, but a lot of plastic dishpans would be better than nothing. And kids could bring in special things from home to observe.

"For a science table, I'm just going to push a couple of extra desks together."

On Time

Problem: "I'm supposed to cover all these things each week. There's the math and reading groups, and writing and spelling, social studies; a specialist comes to do art, and another to do music, and then there is gym three times a week. Where am I supposed to fit in science?"

Solution: "I'm starting to realize how much this science work overlaps other curriculum areas. Kids at work on science are doing interesting writing, and drawing; sometimes there's reading or math as well. Maybe I can just use some writing time for observation, or work with the art teacher to try a unit on scientific drawing."

I was impressed that no matter how large the obstacles seemed, teachers who wished to change the way they were working could come up with a way to make a change. Some wanted to institute small and specific changes: "I'm just going to try this observation idea with one textbook chapter—then I'll see"; "I realize I've given kids a chance to show what they know through writing, but that's not everyone's strength! I'm going to expand the ways kids can share understanding." Others wanted sweeping changes: "I'm going to get rid of my desk, rearrange the other furniture in my classroom, and take it from there!" Most chose small steps and those were big enough!

Running a Science Meeting for the first time, using children's questions to stimulate discussion, and encouraging individualized work represent exciting changes, which may require us to redefine roles, develop new skills, and experiment with teaching strategies. Even the small steps we take toward improving our science programs can bring about important changes. And just like the children, we can only begin where we are.

Bibliography

1 • Curriculum Guides and Units for Teachers

2 • Reference Books for the Classroom

3 • Field Guides

4 • Where to Get Materials, Supplies, Kits, and Information

5 • Films and Videos

6 • Caring for Animals in the Classroom

7 • Fieldwork

8 • Observing Children and Interpreting Work

9 • Special Needs

10 • Integrating Literature

11 • Integrating Art

12 • Magazines for Children

13 • Newsletters and Periodicals for Teachers

14 • Teaching

15 • Evaluation

16 • Developmental Theory and Applications

17 • Beginning Writing

18 • Adult Learners

1 • Curriculum Guides and Units for Teachers

Two outstanding series of guides for teachers are the ESS units and the Macdonald Educational Science 5/13 series. Both provide ideas for developmentally appropriate and active explorations in science. They do not prescribe work; they provide possible directions and examples of what other teachers and children have done. Teachers will use this material in their own ways. Herein lies the excitement and power of this work, and the reason you may want to locate teachers experienced with these approaches if you are new to them.

The Elementary Science Study (ESS) Curriculum. Newton, Mass.: Educational Development Center. More than fifty ESS curriculum units were developed. Many of these are available from Delta Education,* Nashua, N.H., including

Attribute Games and Problems

Balloons and Gases

Batteries and Bulbs

Behavior of Mealworms

Bones

Brine Shrimp

Clay Boats

Colored Solutions

Drops, Streams, and Containers

Earthworms

Eggs and Tadpoles

Gasses and Airs

Growing Seeds

Heating and Cooling

Kitchen Physics

Mapping

Mystery Powders

Peas and Particles

Pendulums

Primary Balancing

Sink or Float

Small Things

Ennever, Len, Wynne Harlen, and others. 1972. *With objectives in mind: Guide to science 5–13*. London: Macdonald Educational Ltd.

Please note that an asterisk(*) after a name indicates more complete address information available in section 4.

Macdonald Science 5/13 titles. Write to Teachers' Laboratory.*

    Change: Stages 1 and 2

    Change: Stage 3

    Children and Plastics: Stages 1 and 2, and Background

    Coloured Things: Stages 1 and 2

    Early Experiences

    Holes, Gaps, and Cavities: Stages 1 and 2

    Like and Unlike: Stages 1, 2, and 3

    Metals: Background information

    Metals: Stages 1 and 2

    Minibeasts: Stages 1 and 2

    Ourselves: Stages 1 and 2

    Science from Toys: Stages 1 and 2, and Background

    Science, Models, and Toys: Stage 3

    Structures and Forces: Stages 1 and 2

    Structures and Forces, Stage 3

    Time, Stages 1 and 2, and Background

    Trees, Stages 1 and 2

    Using the Environment
    1. Early explorations
    2. Investigations—Part 1; Part 2
    3. Tackling problems—Part 1; Part 2
    4. Ways and means

    With Objectives in Mind

    Working with Wood, Background information

    Working with Wood, Stages 1 and 2

Other excellent guides include

Beaty, Seddon Kelly, and Karen DeRusha. 1987. *Sand and Water*. A Curriculum Guide. Early Education Curriculum.

Hill, Dorothy M. 1977. *Mud, sand, and water*. Washington, D.C.: National Association for the Education of Young Children.

Sprung, Barbara, Merle Froschl, and Patricia B. Campbell. 1985. *What will happen if . . . Young children and the scientific method*. New York: Educational Equity Concepts.

Teaching Primary Science Series. Write to Teacher's Laboratory* for information on the following.

    Aerial Models

    Candles

    Fibres and Fabrics

    Introduction and Guide to Teaching Primary Science

    Mirrors and Magnifiers

Musical Instruments

Paints and Materials

Science from Waterplay

Science from Wood

Seeds and Seedlings

2 ● Reference Books for the Classroom

Since so many excellent science books for children are available, I use the following guidelines to limit what I buy and borrow.

Short books on a relatively narrow topic are usually easier for children to use than lengthy, encyclopedia-type books. I search for books that are both interesting and beautiful, with texts that present information understandably and accurately. Photographs and attractive or informative illustrations are important teachers; they can show us new aspects of things we've actually observed and provide us with detail or variety beyond what the classroom can supply. Good reference books are engaging and inspire further work for both me and the children. I buy books connected to topics I plan to introduce during the year, as well as books on everyday things that children are likely to encounter on their own.

My favorite reference book series, by Oxford Scientific Films, includes the following titles:

Bees and Honey

Common Frog

Dragonflies

Grey Squirrel

Harvest Mouse

House Mouse

Jellyfish and Other Sea Creatures

Mosquito

The Butterfly Cycle

The Chicken and the Egg

The Spider's Web

The Stickleback Cycle

The Wild Rabbit

While some of these titles are no longer in print, they are well worth a book search. For a list of those available, write: G.P. Putnam's Sons, 200 Madison Avenue, New York, NY 10016.

Other Series and Individual Titles

Ladybird Series 651. Auburn, Me.: Ladybird Books, 19 Omni Circle. Titles in this series are

Animals and How They Live

Birds and How They Live

Learning about Insects and Small Animals

Life of the Honey-bee

Nature Takes Shape

Plants and How They Grow

Prehistoric Animals and Fossils

The Story of the Ant

The Story of the Spider

Books in the Practical Puffins series are full of projects and activities for children. Published by Puffin Books, a division of Penquin Books, New York. Titles include

Bicycles

Body tricks

Bottles and cans

Carpentry

Cooking

Constructions

Cover-ups

Exploring

Gardening

Kites

Messages

Out in the wilds

Presents

Strange things

The *Animal Habitats* series by Oxford Scientific Films (Milwaukee, Wisc.: Gareth Stevens, Inc.). Eight titles deal with familiar animals.

The National Geographic Society* has published a series called *Books for Young Explorers* with excellent photographs and simple text.

The *Discovering Nature* series now includes nine titles about familiar animals with more in preparation. Photographs are from Oxford Scientific Films. Write to the Bookwright Press, 387 Park Avenue South, New York, NY 10016.

Alfred A. Knopf (New York, N.Y.) has published a new eight-book series, *Eyewitness Books*. The books contain many photographs, presented in a museum display–like fashion, with labels, captions, and informative text.

The *Lerner Natural Science* series (Minneapolis, Minn.: Lerner Publications) contains twenty-eight books about different animals and plants. Several are recipients of the New York Academy of Science's Children's Science Book Award. Highly recommended. Write to Carolina Biological* or First Avenue Editions, 241 First Avenue North, Minneapolis, MN 55401.

The *Living Science* series (London and Basingstoke: Macmillan Education, Ltd.) includes four titles about familiar insects and other small animals. These are short books with photographs and ideas for experiments and record keeping.

The *New True Books* are a series including more than one hundred titles on plants, animals, physical science topics, and machinery. These books are distributed by Children's Press, 1224 West Van Buren Street, Chicago, IL 60607.

The *Usborne First Nature Books* (Tulsa, Okla.: EDC Publishing) include seven titles with simple text and beautiful illustrations.

Bentley, W. A., and W. J. Humphreys. 1962. *Snow crystals*. New York: Dover Publications.

Brenner, Barbara. 1973. *If you were an ant*. New York: Harper and Row.

Carpenter, Mimi Gregoire. 1981. *What the sea left behind*. Camden, Me.: Down East Books.

Cristini, Ermanno, and Luigi Puricelli. 1981. *In my garden*. Salzburg, Austria: Verlag Neugebauer.

————. 1983. *In the woods*. Salzburg, Austria: Verlag Neugebauer.

————. 1984. *In the pond*. Salzburg, Austria: Verlag Neugebauer.

Darby, Gene. 1957. *What is a frog?* New York: Scholastic Book Services.

Feininger, Andreas. [1977] 1984. *Leaves*. New York: Dover Publications.

Freedman, Russell. 1978. *Getting born*. New York: Holiday House.

Goor, Ron, and Nancy Goor. 1981. *Shadows here, there, and everywhere*. New York: Crowell.

Grillone, Lisa, and Joseph Gennaro. 1978. *Small worlds close up*. New York: Crown.

Gunderson, Harvey. 1964. *The wonder of monarchs*. A Young Owl Book. New York: Holt, Rinehart and Winston.

Heller, Ruth. 1984. *Plants that never ever bloom*. New York: Grosset and Dunlap.

Hogeweg, Martin, and Hans Dorrestign. 1979. *The Weasel*. Woodbury, N.Y.: Barron's.

Howell, Ruth. 1973. *Splash and flow*. Photos by Arline Strong. New York: Atheneum.

Jacobson, Morris K., and David R. Franz. 1980. *Wonders of snails and slugs*. New York: Dodd, Mead.

Kalas, Sybille, and Klaus Kalas. 1987. *The beaver family book*. Salzburg, Austria: Neugebauer.

Kellin, Sally Moffet. 1968. *A book of snails*. Photos by Martin Iger. New York: Young Scott Books.

Lane, Margaret. 1981. *The squirrel*. New York: Dial.

Lauber, Patricia. 1981. *Seeds. Pop stick glide.* Photos by Jerome Wexler. New York: Crown.

————. 1987. *What's hatching out of that egg?* New York: Crown.

Livaudais, Madeleine, and Robert Dunne. 1972. *The skeleton book—an inside look at animals.* New York: Scholastic Book Services.

McPhee Gribble Publishers. 1978. *Smells—things to do with them.* A Puffin Book in the Practical Puffins series. New York: Penguin Books Australia Ltd.

Nash, Pamela. 1983. *The frog.* Cleveland: Modern Curriculum.

Nilsson, Lennart. 1975. *How was I born?* New York: Delacorte.

Owen, Jennifer. 1984. *Mysteries and marvels of insect life.* London: Osborne Publishing Ltd.

Patent, Dorothy Hinshaw. 1986. *Mosquitoes.* New York: Holiday House.

Paull, John. 1980. *The story of the spider.* Loughborough, England: Ladybird Books.

Selsam, Millicent E., and Ronald Goor. 1981. *Backyard insects.* New York: Scholastic Book Services.

Shuttlesworth, Dorothy, and Su Zan Noguchi Swain. 1959. *The story of spiders.* Garden City, N.Y.: Garden City Books.

————. 1964. *The story of ants.* Garden City, N.Y.: Doubleday.

Van Soelen, Philip. 1979. *Cricket in the grass.* San Francisco: Sierra Club Books; New York: Charles Scribner's Sons.

Watts, Barrie. 1985. *Butterfly and caterpillar.* Morristown, N.J.: Silver Burdett Company.

Webster, David. 1974. *Let's find out about mosquitoes.* New York: Franklin Watts.

World Book. 1981. *The bug book.* 1981 Childcraft Annual. Chicago: Childcraft International.

Zubrowski, Bernie. 1979. *Bubbles.* A Children's Museum Activity Book. Boston: Little, Brown.

————. 1981. *Messing around with baking chemistry.* A Children's Museum Activity Book. Boston: Little, Brown.

————. 1981. *Messing around with water pumps and siphons.* A Children's Museum Activity Book. Boston: Little, Brown.

3 ● Field Guides

So many beautiful field guides are now on the market! Although I don't emphasize identification as an end product, I do fill our classroom shelves with field guides of various kinds. The children and I use them frequently to answer specific questions (what is it? where does it live?) or just to pore over, soaking up a sense of the astonishing diversity of living and nonliving things in our world. A guide to field guides follows.

Beginner Guides

Many "beginner guides" identifying the most familiar species are designed with fewer pages and simple format to facilitate their use by students. My favorites are

Audubon Society Pocket Guides. New York: Knopf.

Golden Guides. New York: Golden Press.

Peterson's First Guides. Boston: Houghton Mifflin.

Standard Field Guides

"Standard" field guides identify many kinds of living and nonliving things. They are written for adults, but are also interesting and useful for children, especially when adult help is available. Series I've used in the classroom include

Audubon Society Field Guides. New York: Knopf.

Golden Field Guides. New York: Golden Press.

Peterson Field Guides. Boston: Houghton Mifflin.

Field Guides. New York: Simon and Schuster.

Guides for Amateur Naturalists

A "new breed" of field guides, designed for amateur naturalists, deal with fewer species in more detail than traditional guides. Many focus on the commonplace and provide fascinating information about life histories, behavior, and relationship to humans.

Babcock, Harold L. 1971. *Turtles of the northeastern United States*. New York: Dover.

Brown, Lauren. 1986. *Weeds in winter*. New York: W. W. Norton.

Cronin, Edward W., Jr. 1986. *Getting started in birdwatching*. Boston: Houghton Mifflin.

Epple, Anne Orth. 1983. *The amphibians of New England*. Camden, Me.: Down East Books.

Garber, Steven D. 1987. *The urban naturalist*. Wiley Science Editions. New York: John Wiley and Sons.

Harrison, Kit, and George Harrison. 1985. *America's favorite backyard wildlife*. New York: Simon and Schuster.

Headstrom, Richard. 1984. *Suburban wildlife*. Englewood Cliffs, N.J.: Prentice Hall.

Lawrence, Gale. 1984. *A field guide to the familiar: Learning to observe the natural world*. New York: Prentice Hall.

———. 1986. *The indoor naturalist: Observing the world of nature inside your home*. New York: Prentice Hall.

Mitchell, John Hanson. 1985. *A field guide to your own back yard*. New York: W. W. Norton.

Nicholls, Richard E. 1977. *The Running Press book of turtles*. Philadelphia, Penn.: Running Press.

Stokes, Donald W. 1976. *A guide to nature in winter. Northeast and north central North America*. Boston: Little, Brown.

————. 1979. *A guide to the behavior of common birds*. Boston: Little, Brown.

————. 1983. *A guide to observing insect lives*. Boston: Little, Brown.

Stokes, Donald, and Lillian Stokes. 1987. *The bird feeder book*. Boston: Little, Brown.

4 ● Where to Get Materials, Supplies, Kits, and Information

The books and catalogs listed below supply all kinds of things, from mealworms to microscopes to rubber tubing and books. Use them to get ideas, locate supplies, and discover things you didn't even know you needed.

National Science Resources Center. 1988. *Science for children: Resources for teachers*. Washington, D.C.: National Academy Press. Order from National Academy Press, 2101 Constitution Avenue NW, Washington, DC 20418, $7.95 each—all orders prepaid.

Science for Children is an outstanding resource guide. Curriculum materials and supplementary resources are described; prices and suppliers are included. A section of ''Sources of Information and Assistance'' lists museums and science centers, professional organizations, curriculum projects, publishers and suppliers.

Saul, Wendy, with Alan R. Newman. 1986. *Science fare: An illustrated guide and catalog of toys, books, and activities for kids*. New York: Harper and Row.

Science Fare is an unusual resource book that is organized by topic and includes ideas about teaching as well as sources of books and supplies.

The Teacher's Laboratory, Inc. (214 Main Street, P.O. Box 6480, Brattleboro, VT 05301-6480, 802-254-3457) carries many of the Macdonald Science 5/13 titles, as well as other good books on teaching science.

Order ESS guides and kits from Delta Education, Inc. (P.O. Box M, Nashua, NH 03061, (800) 258-1302, 603-889-8899).

The Cornell University Laboratory of Ornithology (Sapsucker Woods Road, Ithaca, NY 14850) publishes a catalog of books and records. Slides (35mm transparencies) of birds are also available.

Carolina Biological Supply Company (2700 York Road, Burlington, NC 27216-9988, 800-334-5551) catalog contains an enormous variety of items—laboratory equipment, an extensive selection of books, live plants and animals, and preserved specimens. Other dealers of equipment or specimens include Connecticut Valley Biological Supply Company, Inc. (Valley Road, P.O. Box 326, Southampton, MA 01073, 800-282-7757, 800-628-7748); National Geographic Educational Services Catalog (National Geographic Society, 17th and M Streets NW, Washington, DC 20036, 202-857-7000); and Nasco (901 Janesville Avenue, Fort Atkinson, WI 53538, 800-558-9595).

Jerryco (601 Linden Place, Evanston, IL 60202, (312)475-8440) deals in surplus of all sorts. Over the years I've bought their test tubes, brass gears, magnets, motors, lenses, tubing, and countless other items.

In Massachusetts, the Children's Museum (300 Congress Street, Boston, MA 02210, 617-426-8855) and the Museum of Science (Science Park, Boston, MA 02114, 617-723-2500), both in Boston, have rental kits available for teachers. Kit rental can be a way to acquire unusual or expensive materials (bones, bird mounts, etc.). Check local museums and nature centers to find out what is available in your area.

The *Franklin Watts* (387 Park Avenue South, New York, NY 10016) *Catalog of Books for Readers Grades K–12* contains many excellent science titles.

5 • Films and Videos

I use films and videos to expand upon our observations. My favorite ones, the film loops developed by ESS, are short (several minutes in length), silent, and can be set up for independent viewing by individuals or small groups. Topics relate to ESS units (for example, there are time-lapse sequences of tadpoles developing into frogs and beans sprouting and wonderful footage of pond animals searching for food). Sadly, these film loops are no longer being marketed, but ask around, and maybe you will find one in your school, a local university, or nearby museum.

Some of the catalogs listed in the previous section sell films and videos. Your local extension service or a nearby college may also be able to help.

6 ● Caring for Animals in the Classroom

The following books offer detailed instructions on housing and feeding many of the animals commonly sold in pet stores, discovered on field trips, or brought to school in the morning in mayonnaise jars. They are helpful references in specific, as well as general, situations. The various stances of the authors on issues like collecting, keeping wild animals in captivity, and pet breeding can help us to develop values and standards for our classrooms.

American Humane Society. 1977. *Small Mammal Care*. Pamphlet. Boston: American Humane Education Society.

Axelrod, Herbert. 1985. *Dr. Axelrod's atlas of freshwater aquarium fishes*. Neptune, N.J.: TFH Publications.

Breen, John F. 1974. *Encyclopedia of reptiles and amphibians*. Neptune, N.J.: TFH Publications.

Headstrom, Richard. 1964. *Adventures with freshwater animals*. New York: Dover.

————. 1982. *Adventures with insects*. New York: Dover.

Hickman, Mae, and Maxine Guy. 1973. *Care of the wild feathered and furred: A guide to wildlife handling and care*. 1973. Santa Cruz, Calif.: Unity Press.

Pyrom, Jay. 1987. *Complete introduction to frogs and toads*. Neptune, N.J.: TFH Publications.

Ricciuti, Edward R. 1971. *Shelf pets: How to take care of small wild animals*. New York: Harper and Row.

Simon, Seymour. 1975. *Pets in a jar: Collecting and caring for small animals*. New York: Penguin.

Snedigar, Robert. 1963. *Our small native animals: Their habits and care*. New York: Dover.

7 ● Fieldwork

Fieldwork can be a wonderful part of elementary school science study. Many kinds of books help us as we move our work outdoors—field guides, books of nature activities for children, books about specific plants, animals or resources.

The Macdonald Science 5/13 series contains a number of excellent titles dealing specifically with field studies. All provide us with examples of places to investigate (beginning with the school yard), questions to help focus observation and exploration, techniques for indoor and outdoor work, and photographs of children's work. *Early Explorations* and *Ways and Means* (numbers 1 and 4 in Using the Environment) include a breakdown of the teacher's role in organizing fieldwork. In addition, many other Macdonald titles connect classroom and outdoor work (for example, *Minibeasts* and *Trees*).

Other books with good ideas for outdoor work are

Caduto, Michael. 1985. *Pond and brook: A guide to nature study in freshwater environments*. Englewood Cliffs, N.J.: Prentice Hall.

Durrell, Gerald. 1986. *A practical guide for the amateur naturalist*. New York: Knopf.

Harris, Melville. 1971. *Environmental studies*. New York: Citation Press.

Headstrom, Richard. 1963. *Adventures with insects*. New York: Dover.

Mitchell, John, and the Massachusetts Audubon Society. 1980. *The curious naturalist*. Englewood Cliffs, N.J.: Prentice Hall.

Mitchell, Lucy Sprague. 1971. *Young geographers*. New York: Bank Street College of Education.

Russell, Helen Ross. 1972. *Small worlds: A field trip guide*. Boston: Little, Brown.

————. 1973. *Ten-minute field trips: A teacher's guide—using the school grounds for environmental studies*. Chicago, Ill.: J. G. Ferguson.

————. Other titles include *City Critters; Clarion the Killdeer; Soil: A Field Trip Guide; The True Book of Buds; The True Book of Springtime Seeds; Winter: A Field Trip Guide; Winter Search Party*.

Simon, Seymour. 1970. *Science in a vacant lot*. New York: Viking.

Sisson, Edith A., and the Massachusetts Audubon Society. 1982. *Nature with children of all ages*. New York: Prentice Hall.

Wensberg, Katherine. 1966. *Experiences with living things—an introduction to ecology for five to eight year olds*. Boston: Beacon Press.

Wilson, Jennifer Bauer. 1986. *A naturalist's teaching manual: Activities and ideas for teaching natural history*. Englewood Cliffs, N.J.: Prentice Hall.

8 ● Observing Children—Interpreting Work

As children go about their work in science, their behaviors and products tell us about their development, understanding, learning style, interests, and needs.

The works of Arnold Gesell and others at the Gesell Institute explain about children's neuromotor development and behavior. Teachers who have received Gesell training will find *Scoring Notes—The Developmental Examination* helpful. Also, see *The Child from Five to Ten*.

Cohen, Dorothy H. and Virginia Stern. 1978. *Observing and recording the behavior of young children*. New York: Teachers College Press. A clear and useful introduction to observing children in the classroom.

Gardner, Howard. 1985. *Frames of mind: The theory of multiple intelligence*. New York: Basic. This book presents Howard Gardner's theory of multiple intelligences.

Gesell, Arnold, Frances Ilg, and others. 1977. *The child from five to ten*. Rev. ed. New York: Harper and Row.

Ilg, Frances. 1985. *Scoring notes—The developmental examination*. Rev. ed. New Haven, Conn.: Gesell Institute of Human Development.

Wadsworth, Barry J. 1978. *Piaget for the classroom teacher*. New York: Longman. (Describes Piaget's theory of cognitive development and includes a chapter on assessment.)

Sime, Mary. 1973. *A child's eye view*. New York: Harper and Row. Another book that can help teachers to understand some aspects of Piaget's work.

For information about children's art work, see

DiLeo, Joseph H. 1970. *Young children and their drawings*. New York: Brunner/Mazel.

Lowenfeld, Viktor, and W. Lambert Brittain. 1970. *Creative and mental growth*. 5th ed. New York: Macmillan.

Gardner, Howard. 1980. *Artful Scribbles: The Significance of Children's' Drawings*. New York: Basic.

9 • Special Needs

I have come across a small number of titles that describe the work of special needs children in science or discuss ways to adapt activities and units to meet special needs. My favorite, *The Logic of Action—Young Children at Work* by Francis Pockman Hawkins (Boulder, Colo: Colorado Associated University Press, 1986), describes the author's work with a group of deaf three- and four-year-olds. It is an excellent account of children at work and the thoughts and actions of their teachers.

A thorough and thoughtful book on working with students with a variety of special needs is Helenmarie Hofman and Kenneth Ricker's *Sourcebook: Science Education and the Physically Handicapped* (Washington, D.C.: National Science Teacher's Association, 1979). Good for teachers of older students, this book helps us try to understand the real abilities of our students and develop appropriate teaching practices.

The following books describe projects developed for special needs students or contain specific reference to such students:

See *Connect* (newsletter), listed in section 13.

Downs, Gary, and Jack Gerlovich. 1983. *Science safety for elementary teachers*. Ames, Iowa: Iowa State University Press.

Oryx Science Bibliographies. 1986. *Science education*. vol. 6. Phoenix, Ariz.: Oryx Press.

Waxter, Julia. 1981. *The science cookbook*. Belmont, Calif.: David S. Lake.

10 ● Integrating Literature

Many teachers like to integrate literature and science study. The approach can be as simple as reading *The Lady and the Spider* to children who have noticed a spider on the way in from the playground, or as involved as helping students to tackle *Charlotte's Web* in reading group, sorting spider fact from fiction as part of their work on a class theme. The following books, grouped by topic, may be suitable.

Spiders

Arkhurst, Joyce Cooper. 1987. *The adventures of spider*. New York: Scholastic Books.

Carle, Eric. 1985. *The very busy spider*. New York: Philomel Books.

Chenery, Janet. 1969. *Wolfie*. New York: Harper and Row.

Freschet, Bernice. 1972. *The web in the grass*. New York: Charles Scribner's Sons.

Lexau, Joan M. 1976. *The spider makes a web*. New York: Hastings House.

McNulty, Faith. 1986. *The lady and the spider*. A Harper Trophy Book. New York: Harper and Row.

White, E. B. 1952. *Charlotte's web*. New York: Harper and Row.

Birds

Atwater, Richard, and Florence Atwater. 1986. *Mr. Popper's penguins*. Dell: New York.

Byars, Betsy. 1972. *The house of wings*. New York: Viking.

George, Jean Craighead. 1975. *My side of the mountain*. New York: Dutton.

——. 1980. *The cry of the crow*. New York: Harper and Row.

Mowat, Farley. 1981. *Owls in the family*. New York: Bantam Books.

Whelen, Gloria. 1987. *Next spring an oriole*. New York: Random House.

White, E. B. 1973. *The trumpet of the swan*. New York: Harper and Row.

Yolen, Jane. 1987. *Owl moon*. New York: Philomel Books.

Mammals

Aesop. 1965. *Aesop's fables*. Illustrated by Eric Carle. Mount Vernon, N.Y.: Peter Pauper Press.

Byars, Betsy. 1968. *The midnight fox*. New York: Viking.

Dahl, Ronald. 1970. *Fantastic Mr. Fox*. New York: Bantam.

George, Jean Craighead. 1972. *Julie of the wolves*. New York: Harper and Row.

Hogeweg, Martin and Hans Dorrestign. 1979. *The weasel*. Woodbury, N.Y.: Barrons.

Kipling, Rudyard. 1967. *How the leopard got his spots and other stories*. New York: Grolier Society.

Lobel, Arnold. 1983. *Mouse soup*. New York: Harper and Row.

White, E. B. 1945. *Stuart Little*. New York: Harper and Row.

Insects

Carle, Eric. 1977. *The grouchy ladybug*. New York: Thomas Y. Crowell.

George, Jean Craighead. 1974. *All upon a sidewalk*. New York: E. P. Dutton.

Jones, Chuck. 1984. *The cricket in Times Square* (and sequels). Nashville, Tenn.: Ideal.

Reptiles

Holling, Holling Clancy. 1951. *Minn of the Mississippi*. Boston: Houghton Mifflin.

Amphibians

Lobel, Arnold. 1972. *Frog and toad together*. New York: Harper and Row.

————. 1979. *Frog and toad are friends*. New York: Harper and Row.

————. 1984. *Days with frog and toad*. New York: Harper and Row.

————. 1984. *Frog and toad all year*. New York: Harper and Row.

11 ● Integrating Art

Drawing, painting, and modeling are ways to record what we see; they are also tools that help us to see. To learn new art techniques that can enhance our ability to observe and represent, refer to

Leslie, Clare Walker. 1980. *Nature drawing—a tool for learning*. Englewood Cliffs, N.J.: Prentice Hall.

————. 1984. *The art of field sketching*. New York: Prentice Hall.

A wonderful book about the processes of art and children's products that includes examples of how art and science can be combined is

Cohen, Elaine Pear, and Ruth Straus Gainer. 1984. *Art: Another language for learning*. New York: Schocken Books.

12 ● Magazines for Children

Several good magazines for children have been written with a science focus. I often clip pictures and articles on particular subjects and bind them for our reference collection, and of course, children find new magazine arrivals exciting to explore. I use

National Geographic World. Washington, D.C.: National Geographic Society.* Twelve issues per year.

Ranger Rick. Vienna, VA: National Wildlife Federation (8925 Leesburg Pike, Vienna, VA 22184-0001). Twelve issues per year.

Your Big Back Yard. Vienna, VA: National Wildlife Federation (8925 Leesburg Pike, Vienna, VA 22184-0001). Twelve issues per year.

Zoobooks. San Diego, Calif.: Wildlife Education, Ltd. (930 West Washington Street, San Diego, CA 92103). Ten issues per year.

Magazines published for adults appeal to older child readers, or even younger children if assisted.

Audubon. New York: National Audubon Society (950 Third Avenue, New York, NY 10022). Six issues per year.

International Wildlife. Washington, D.C.: National Wildlife Federation (see above). Six issues per year.

National Geographic. Washington, D.C.: National Geographic Society.* Twelve issues per year.

National Wildlife. Washington, D.C.: National Wildlife Federation (see above). Six issues per year.

Science News. Washington, D.C.: Science Service, Inc. (1719 N Street NW, Washington, DC 20036). Weekly.

13 ● Newsletters and Periodicals for Teachers

These publications inform us about the work of other teachers and about current research in education. The first group deals with science education specifically, the second with various aspects of teaching.

Science Teaching

National Science Resources Center Newsletter. Smithsonian Institution (Washington, DC 20560).

Science Education News. A newsletter from Organization for Science and Technology Education, 1333 H Street NW, Washington, DC 20005.

Connect. The Newsletter of Practical Science and Math for K–8 Teachers. Available from the Teacher's Laboratory.*

Science and Children. National Science Teachers Association journal for elementary and middle school teachers. National Science Teachers Association, 1742 Connecticut Avenue NW, Washington, DC 20009.

The Science Teacher. National Science Teachers Association (see above).

Science Scope. A quarterly for middle/junior high science teachers. National Science Teachers Association (see above).

Teaching

Pathways. A Forum for Progressive Educators. Center for Teaching and Learning, Box 8158, University of North Dakota, Grand Forks, ND 48202.

14 ● Teaching

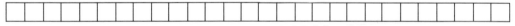

These are books to turn to again and again, for ideas, insight, and inspiration.

Carson, Rachael. 1956. *The sense of wonder*. (Photographs by Charles Pratt, 1965). New York: Harper and Row.

Charney, R., M. Clayton, M. Finer, J. Lord, and C. Wood. 1984. *A notebook for teachers*. Greenfield, Mass.: Northeast Foundation for Children.

Duckworth, Eleanor. 1978. *The African primary science program: An evaluation and extended thoughts*. Grand Forks, N.D.: North Dakota Study Group on Evaluation.

———. 1987. *"The having of wonderful ideas" and other essays on teaching and learning*. New York: Teachers College Press.

Harlen, Wynne. 1985. *Teaching and learning primary science*. New York: Teachers College Press.

———, ed. 1985. *Primary science—taking the plunge*. Portsmouth, N.H.: Heinemann Educational Books.

Hawkins, David. 1974. *The informed vision: Essays on learning and human nature*. New York: Agathon Press. "Messing About in Science," included in this collection, is a must!

Hawkins, Francis Pockman. 1986. *The logic of action—Young children at work*. Boulder, Colo.: Colorado Associated University Press.

Holt, Bess, and Gene Holt. 1977. *Science with young children*. Washington, D.C.: National Association for the Education of Young Children.

Mitchell, Lucy Sprague. 1951. *Our children and our schools*. New York: Simon and Schuster.

———. 1971. *Young geographers*. New York: Bank Street College of Education.

Pratt, Carolyn. 1990. *I learn from children*. New York: Harper Collins.

Rogers, V. R., ed. 1970. *Teaching in the British primary school*. London: Macmillan Education.

Silberman, Charles E., ed. 1973. *The open classroom reader*. New York: Vintage Books.

15 ● Evaluation

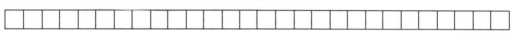

Carini, Patricia F. 1979. *The art of seeing and the visibility of the person*. Grand Forks, N.D.: North Dakota Study Group on Evaluation.

———. 1988. *Another way of looking: Views on evaluation and education* (Two talks). North Bennington, Vt.: Prospect Archive and Center for Education and Research.

Duckworth, Eleanor. 1978. *The African primary science program: An evaluation and extended thoughts*. Grand Forks, N.D.: North Dakota Study Group on Evaluation.

Eisner, Elliot. 1979. *The educational imagination*. New York: Macmillan.

———. 1982. *Cognition and curriculum: A basis for deciding what to teach*. White Plains, N.Y.: Longman.

Harlen, Wynne. 1985. *Teaching and learning primary science*. New York: Teacher's College Press.

16 ● Developmental Theory and Applications

Understanding child development helps us to plan the classroom environment, choose appropriate topics and ways of working, and know what to expect of our students.

For a survey of different developmental theories, see

Crain, William C. 1985. *Theories of development—concepts and applications*. Englewood Cliffs, N.J.: Prentice Hall.

These theoretical works have particular relevance to classroom teachers:

Erikson, Erik H. 1963. *Childhood and society*. Rev. ed. New York: W.W. Norton.

Gesell, Arnold, Frances Ilg, et al. 1977. *The child from five to ten*. Rev. ed. New York: Harper and Row.

Some of Piaget's own writings that may be of interest are

Piaget, Jean. 1966. *The child's conception of physical causality*. Totowa, N.J.: Littlefield, Adams and Company.

———. 1976. *To understand is to invent*. New York: Penguin Books.

For a practical and accessible description of Piaget's work as it applies to teaching, see

Wadsworth, Barry J. 1978. *Piaget for the classroom teacher*. New York: Longman.

———. 1979. *Piaget's theory of cognitive development*. New York: Longman.

The *UNESCO Handbook for Science Teachers* 1980 (Unipub, 345 Park Avenue, New York, NY 10010, 1980) discusses the work of Piaget and others and implications for science teaching.

An analysis of the way children develop and learn is provided by Dorothy Cohen:

Cohen, Dorothy H. 1988. *The learning child*. New York: Schocken Books.

17 • Beginning Writing

Throughout this book I have discussed and shown examples of children using "invented spelling." In this approach, children do not limit their written expression to words they can spell correctly; they write the sounds as they hear them. If you are new to this approach and would like to find out more, try

Clay, Marie M. 1975. *What did I write?—beginning writing behavior*. Portsmouth, N.H.: Heinemann Educational Books.

Graves, Donald. 1983. *Writing: Teachers and children at work*. Portsmouth, N.H.: Heinemann Educational Books.

Newman, Judith. 1984. *The craft of children's writing*. Portsmouth, N.H.: Heinemann Educational Books.

Temple, Charles, Ruth Nathan, Nancy Burris, and Francis Temple. 1988. *The beginnings of writing*. 1982. 2d ed. Boston: Allyn and Bacon.

18 ● Adult Learners

As teachers, we may be looking for a way to start to explore and gain confidence in our abilities to observe and discover. Or we may enjoy engaging in scientific activity and wish to continue our development. Many of the books already cited will help us on our way. In addition, the titles below deal specifically with adults as learners in science.

Science Anxiety is a very readable text that describes ways scientists work, science anxiety, links between science and the arts, and ways we can work to overcome science anxiety.

Mallow, Jeffry V. 1986. *Science anxiety—fear of science and how to overcome it*. Clearwater, Fla.: H & H Publishing Co.

Inventing density is Eleanor Duckworth's insightful account of a group of adults as they worked to uncover the mystery of sinking and floating. A good look at adult exploration and the work of their teacher in a hands-on classroom.

Duckworth, Eleanor. 1986. *Inventing density*. Grand Forks, N.D.: North Dakota Study Group on Evaluation.

Size and scale, heat, mechanics; some things are hard to understand! How can we break through the "critical barriers" that keep us from making sense of the world around us? See:

Apelman, Maja, David Hawkins, and Philip Morrison. 1985. *Critical Barriers Phenomenon in Elementary Science*. Grand Forks, N.D.: North Dakota Study Group on Evaluation

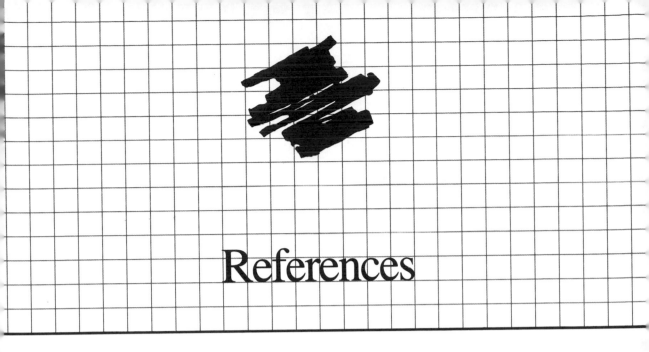

References

Calkins, Lucy. 1986. *The art of teaching writing*. Portsmouth, N.H.: Heinemann.

Carson, Rachel. 1956. *The sense of wonder*. New York: Harper and Row.

Charney, R., M. Clayton, M. Finer, J. Lord, and C. Wood. 1984. *A notebook for teachers*. Greenfield, Mass.: Northeast Foundation for Children.

Duckworth, Eleanor. 1978. *The African primary science program: An evaluation and extended thoughts*. Grand Forks, N.D.: University of North Dakota, Center for Teaching and Learning.

Mitchell, Lucy Sprague. 1971. *Young geographers*. New York: Bank Street College of Education.

National Association for the Education of Young Children. 1988. NAEYC position statement on developmentally appropriate practice in the primary grades, serving five-through eight-year-olds. *Young Children* 33:74.

National Science Resources Center, Smithsonian Institution, National Academy of Sciences. 1988. *NSRC Newsletter* 1(1).

Oxford Scientific Films. 1979. *The chicken and the egg*. New York: Putnam's.

Piaget, Jean. 1976. *To understand is to invent*. New York: Penguin.

Pratt, Carolyn. 1948. *I learn from children*. New York: Simon and Schuster. New edition: New York: HarperCollins, 1990.

Victor, Edward, and Marjorie S. Lerner. ed. 1971. *Readings in science education for the elementary school*. New York: Macmillan.

Wadsworth, Barry J. 1979. *Piaget's Theory of Cognitive Development*. New York: Longman, Inc.

Weiss, Iris R. 1987. *Report of the 1985–86 National Survey of Science and Mathematics Education*. Research Triangle Park, N.C.: Iris R. Weiss Research Triangle Institute.

Appendix A: Worksheet for five- and six-year-olds for long things.

Name of Scientist _____

I looked at _____

———————— A picture of what I saw ————————

I noticed _____

_____

© Heinemann Educational Books. Reprinted by permission.

Appendix B: Worksheet for five- and six-year-olds for tall things.

Name of Scientist _____

I looked at _____

I noticed _____

_____

_____

_____

_____

_____

© Heinemann Educational Books. Reprinted by permission.

Appendix C: Worksheet for seven years and older.

_____ observation

date: _____

I looked at _____

_____

⌐____ A picture of what I saw _____

Here are some things I noticed :

_____

_____

_____

_____

_____

_____

_____

_____

© Heinemann Educational Books. Reprinted by permission.